Strengthening Your Firm:
Strategies for Success

Arthur G. Greene, Editor

Book Two
in the Series

/BA
Law Practice Management Section

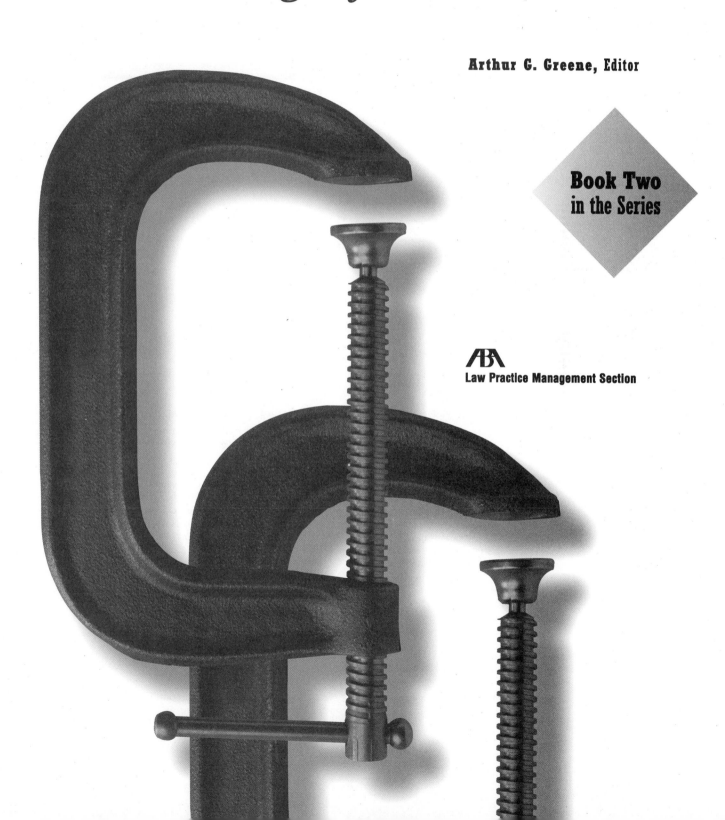

Cover design by David Middleton.

Library of Congress Catalog Card Number 97-73881
ISBN 1-57073-506-9

01 00 99 98 97   5 4 3 2 1

Discounts are available for books ordered in bulk. Special consideration is given to state bars, CLE programs, and other bar-related organizations. Inquire at Book Publishing, American Bar Association, 750 N. Lake Shore Drive, Chicago, Illinois 60611.

Contents

Contents

Contents

Contents

About the Authors

Robert J. Arndt, a former Price Waterhouse partner, has consulted to the legal profession for over thirty years. He now lives on his boat and consults, part-time, to the profession. He is very active in the American Bar Association's Law Practice Management Section, where he now serves as chair of the Leadership Activities Board. He has written numerous books, book chapters, and articles for the section and is a frequent speaker on law office leadership and management, culture renewal, planning, mergers, alternative billing methods, profitability measurement and enhancement, computer technology use, and partner compensation.

Ward Bower is a principal of Altman Weil Pensa, Inc. He heads consulting assignments in law firm management and organization, strategic and partnership planning, and compensation-related issues. He is a former U.S. Army officer and previously worked in industry as a consultant before attending law school. Mr. Bower is co-author of a law office management treatise (published by Matthew Bender & Company) and has authored articles for numerous publications. He is a frequent speaker on law office management-related topics, nationally and internationally. A former Council member and Division Chair of the American Bar Association Law Practice Management Section, Mr. Bower currently serves as a Council member in the Section on General Practice of the International Bar Association. He served for many years on the faculty of the ABA/ICLE Strategic Planning Institute at the University of Michigan Business School. A fellow of the American Bar Foundation and the College of Law Practice Management, he serves as a permanent trustee of The Dickinson School of Law. He chairs the IBA's Standing Committee on Multidisciplinary Practices and serves on its Standing Committee for the U.N. and Other Worldwide Organizations. He is a graduate of Bucknell University and the Dickinson School of Law.

Ezra Tom Clark, Jr. is president of E.T. Clark, Inc., a legal management consulting firm located in Mesa, Arizona. He has been a practicing lawyer and has had extensive experience in managing law firms and providing consulting services to small- and medium-sized firms. He is an active member of the ABA, having served as a committee chairperson, division chairperson, and council member of the Law Practice Management Section. He has written numerous articles for national and state publications on law practice management issues. He is a frequent speaker at local, state, and national programs on law firm management. He has presented CLE seminars or programs in thirty-eight states and provinces in the United States and Canada.

Thomas S. Clay is a senior principal of Altman Weil Pensa, Inc., and heads consulting assignments in law firm management and organization, partner compensation, strategic planning, merger and acquisition, and practice development strategies. Formerly he was vice president and general manager of a venture capital company specializing in the provision of consulting services and financing arrangements to entrepreneurial operations. Mr. Clay writes regularly for national, state, and local publications germane to the legal profession. He is also a frequent lecturer on law firm management issues and has addressed, among others, the American Bar Association's Annual Meeting, the ABA Board of Governors, the National Conference of Bar Presidents and Bar Executives, the Commonwealth Law Conference, the National Association of Law Firm Marketing Administrators' annual conference, the Association of Management Consultants' national conference and numerous regional, state, and local bar conferences. He holds an undergraduate degree in business administration from the University of North Carolina at Chapel Hill as well as a master of business administration in finance degree from Georgia State University.

James D. Cotterman is a senior management consultant with Altman Weil Pensa, Inc., specializing in compensation systems, capitalization, buy-in/buy-out, retirement, profitability analysis, economic forecasting models, turnarounds, mergers, firm documentation, governance, and organizational issues. Before joining Altman Weil Pensa, Mr. Cotterman was manager of acquisitions for a public company in the health care industry, where he specialized in the development, analysis, evaluation, and negotiation of mergers. Mr. Cotterman is a regular contributor to *The Altman Weil Pensa Report to Legal Management,* is on the board of editors of *Accounting for Law Firms,* and is the supervising author for *How to Manage Your Law Office.* His writings have appeared in *American Lawyer, National Law Journal, ABA Legal Management, Legal Economics, The Practical Lawyer,* and state and local bar publications. He has lectured on law firm economics, valuation, retirement, alternative pricing and billing arrangements, and capitalization/debt management for groups such as the Association of Legal Administrators and state and local bar associations. He holds an undergraduate degree in operations management and a master of business administration in accounting degree, both from Syracuse University. A licensed certified public accountant in Pennsylvania, he is a member of the American and Pennsylvania Institutes of Certified Public Accountants.

Daniel J. DiLucchio, Jr., is a principal of Altman Weil Pensa, Inc., and consults on strategic planning, organizational and management studies, process reengineering, human resource management compensation and incentive compensation planning, systems and procedures, and other areas of general law department operations. He serves as the firm's managing principal. Before joining Altman Weil Pensa, Mr. DiLucchio was the director of management for the Pennsylvania Office of the Attorney General. He is a member of the Society for Human Resource Management and has written for *The Corporate Legal Times, National Law Journal, American Lawyer, Barrister,* and *Journal of Collective Negotiations in the Public Sector.* He is a speaker on law office management-related topics and has presented before national, local, and state bar associations, the American Corporate Counsel Association, and the Association of Legal Administrators among others. A fellow of the College of Law Practice Management, he is a graduate of John Carroll University, holds a master of arts in industrial relations from St. Francis College, and has completed his doctoral course work at the University of Pennsylvania.

Peter Giuliani is the Executive Director of the Connecticut-based firm of Cummings & Lockwood. He was formerly a principal and shareholder in the consulting firm of Altman Weil Pensa, Inc., and served as the firm's Chief Financial Officer. Prior to joining Cummings & Lockwood, he had been a full-time consultant to law firms since 1970. Mr. Giuliani has been a frequent speaker at many ABA and ALA national and regional seminars and programs on law office management. He is a principal author of the ALA course on strategic planning and has presented the course to several ALA regional and local chapters. Mr. Giuliani has published many articles and two ABA monographs on law firm management subjects. He is a CPA and a Certified Management Consultant.

Arthur G. Greene, Esq., is a trial lawyer with the sixty-lawyer firm of McLane, Graf, Raulerson & Middleton, Professional Association, in Manchester, New Hampshire, where he was active in the firm's management from 1980 to 1993 as a member of its Management Committee, and for three years as its Managing Partner. He is also affiliated with the AndersonBoyer Group, consultants to the legal profession located in Ann Arbor, Michigan, where he focuses on both practice management and the strategic and financial aspects of maintaining a healthy firm. Mr. Greene is a Fellow of the College of Law Practice Management and serves as Vice-Chair and is a member of the Executive Committee of the ABA's Law Practice Management Section. He has lectured and written on a variety of law firm management topics.

Bruce D. Heintz is a management consultant who has specialized in law firms for twenty years. Mr. Heintz offers his services from

About the Authors

Heintz Consulting, located in Boston. Formerly a partner with Ernst & Young, he started and headed their national legal consulting group. He writes and speaks for the ABA, the Practicing Law Institute, the Institute of Continuing Legal Education, the Association of Legal Administrators, and The American Lawyer conference series. He has been quoted in *Fortune*, the *Wall Street Journal*, and numerous legal profession publications. Mr. Heintz holds degrees from Yale and the Harvard Business School.

Gerry Malone is a consultant with the legal management consulting firm of Hildebrandt and is based out of the Dallas, Texas, office. She is a frequent author, and presently serves on the ABA's Section of Law Practice Management Publishing Board.

Howard L. Mudrick is a certified public accountant based in Hildebrandt's Dallas office who manages assignments for law firms throughout the United States and Canada. As the head of Hildebrandt's Financial Practice Group, he assists law firms in management and financial issues, including financial analysis and planning, long-range planning and organizational structuring, mergers and acquisitions, firm reorganizations, compensation systems, strategic planning, management and structure design and evaluation, and firm retreats. Before joining Hildebrandt, he served as controller of the law firm of Miller & Chevalier, where he also held the position of business manager, and was previously assistant controller at the firm of Arent, Fox, Kintner, Plotkin & Kahn. Mr. Mudrick is co-author of *Anatomy of a Merger—How to Make or Break the Deal* (published by the ABA Law Practice Management Section) and a member of the American Institute of CPAs and the board of editors of *Accounting for Law Firms*. He holds a bachelor of science degree from the University of North Carolina.

Berne Rolston is a graduate of Rutgers University (B.A.) and the University of Southern California (J.D.). He was admitted to the California Bar in 1952. In 1970, he co-founded a law partnership, Fulop & Rolston, which grew from 17 lawyers to the 102-lawyer firm of Fulop & Hardee in 1982, with offices in Beverly Hills, New York City, Newport Beach, and San Francisco. In 1982 he served as General Counsel to and Vice President of Shapell Industries, Inc., (then a New York Stock Exchange Corporation), and as a member of its Board of Directors. Since 1984 he has been practicing privately with offices in Santa Monica, California. Mr. Rolston also assists lawyers and law firms in resolving a variety of legal and business issues. He is also a member of the ABA Law Practice Management Section (since its inception as a standing committee in 1969), and he has lectured before many state and national organizations and authored numerous articles on the subject of law practice management.

Foreword

What makes a law firm run? What is the fuel that powers the engine that delivers legal services to clients? How do the owners maintain the engine to keep it in tip-top shape to maximize its performance? What happens when funny little pings, hints of possible trouble, go unheeded? Is it possible to avoid major breakdowns through regular care and maintenance? If we were talking about an automobile, there would be little dispute that the vehicle would last longer, run better, and break down less frequently with regular service. Doesn't it make sense to say that a law firm can be nurtured and sustained by a program of regular care and maintenance in the same way?

The owners of a new law firm often forget that the shiny new organization they create will not stay healthy and robust without their continuous efforts to sustain it. The firm will not grow or fulfill their expectations unless they regularly fine-tune its engine. And if they ignore signs of trouble in the operation of the firm, they should not be surprised when the organization breaks down.

One difference between a law firm and a car is that a law firm doesn't come with a guarantee. You can't take it back to the dealer if the left-turn signal isn't working. Managing a law firm harkens back to the early days of automobiles when you drove at your own risk and fixed the engine yourself when it broke down. In the same way, keeping a law firm together requires the owners and managers to be organizational mechanics.

This book, *Strengthening Your Firm: Strategies for Success*, edited by Arthur Greene, a law firm partner from New Hampshire, might be viewed as a owner's manual for a law firm. It tells you how to keep the engine running, how to service it, and how to recognize the danger signs. It tells you how to keep the fuel of human energy firing the pistons to make your law firm run. It turns to some of the best minds in the legal profession to offer practical advice on how to keep your law firm going—efficiently and effectively.

While the first book in this series, *Getting Started: Basics for a Successful Law Firm*, dealt with putting together the components of a successful law firm, this book addresses what to do after the firm is up and running. Certainly, many of the startup decisions will have an impact on the way the law firm is run, and, undoubtedly, many of the problems that lead to the ultimate dissolution of the firm exist at the outset. All things being equal, however, there are ways to keep an ongoing practice healthy, and to make a healthy practice healthier. There are even ways to identify danger signs and to take remedial steps.

Mr. Greene and his capable stable of authors, Bob Arndt, Tom Clark, Bruce Heintz, Gerry Malone, Howard Mudrick, Berne Rolston, and Altman Weil Pensa's James Cotterman, Dan DiLucchio, Thomas Clay, Ward Bower, and Peter Giuliani, have put together an outstanding compendium on everything the modern law firm needs to keep it going. I join with LPM Publishing Co-Chairs Robert Conroy and Judith Grubner in encouraging its use to you. Whether you are in a two-lawyer firm or a multi-office megafirm, you will gain insights on how to sustain the organization to which you have dedicated a substantial portion of your professional life.

In the competitive environment of law practice today, keeping the firm going is as challenging as getting it started. With this owner's manual, you have an opportunity to take steps to assure the success of your organization. Take care of it, the way you take care of your car.

> Professor Gary A. Munneke
> Pace University School of Law
> Chair-Elect, Law Practice Management Section

Preface

For many lawyers, "the good old days" were the 1980s. The economy was expanding and most businesses were making money at unprecedented levels. Lawyers were billing hours as fast as they could work them and were expanding their legal staff to meet the growing needs of their clients. Many lawyers thought the good times would never end.

But all good things come to an end, and so did the economy of the 1980s. An economic downturn caused many businesses to take a closer look at their costs and their business practices. Change began to sweep the business world as each company did what was necessary to compete in a global marketplace. While the number of lawyers competing for work continued to grow, the amount of good legal work began to contract. For the first time, it was the client who "controlled the playing field."

Successful-appearing law firms began to fail. Medium-sized firms were considered by many to be on the endangered list. Although some firms continued to do well, others struggled to avoid an irreversible decline. Suddenly, *strengthening the firm* became a challenge. This book is designed to assist the small and medium-sized firms in recognizing and implementing the changes they need to make in order to continue to survive and thrive.

The first book in this law firm partnership series, *Getting Started: Basics for a Successful Law Firm*, addressed issues of setting up a firm and had as its centerpiece a model partnership agreement. It was directed to the new firm, the firm being reorganized, and the firm in need of improved structure. This second volume in the series is a survival guide for the existing firm that seeks to maintain or improve its position. The third book in the series will address taking it apart, or the winding down or dissolution of the firm. This three-book project is designed to cover all phases of a law firm's life cycle.

This series of three partnership books was the idea of a former Chair of the ABA's Section of Law Practice Management Publishing Board, Gary Munneke. Having identified the need for these books and appreciating the dramatic changes that have rocked the profession, Gary assembled an outstanding group of individuals for a one-day think-tank session on the changes that have confronted the profession since 1980. The group came up with a list of twenty-eight changes of significance, and that list became the foundation for the works that followed.

I could not have accepted the responsibility for a three-book series without knowing I would be supported by an outstanding steering committee. The individuals who served in that role are all successful law firm consultants with national reputations. They worked long and hard on this project and deserve the credit for whatever success this book achieves.

Robert J. Arndt is a former Price Waterhouse partner from Anacortes, Washington, who has consulted to the legal profession for over thirty years, is active in the ABA's Section of Law Practice Management, and is the author of numerous law office leadership and management articles.

Ezra Tom Clark Jr. is a lawyer with extensive experience managing and consulting with small- and medium-sized firms in the United States and Canada. He is president of E.T. Clark, Inc., in Mesa, Arizona, and is a frequent speaker on law firm management.

Rick Feferman is a practicing lawyer and law firm consultant from Albuquerque, New Mexico, who is active in the ABA's Section of Law Practice Management as Vice-Chair of the Publishing Board in charge of Acquisitions. He also writes and lectures frequently on law practice management issues.

Gerry Malone is a consultant with the legal management consulting firm of Hildebrandt, based in its Dallas office. She is a frequent author and presently serves on the ABA's Section of Law Practice Management Publishing Board.

These individuals acting as the steering committee for this project have met on numerous occasions and dedicated long hours to developing the design of the book and working with the authors. I thank them for that work, as well as the chapters they authored. I also thank each of the other chapter authors for sharing with us their expertise and making an important contribution to this book: Howard L. Mudrick, Berne Rolston, Bruce D. Heintz, and Altman Well Pensa's James Cotterman, Dan DiLucchio, Thomas Clay, Ward Bower, and Peter Giuliani.

The steering committee could not have completed this project without the support and advice of Gary Munneke, who saw the need for the partnership series and made it happen; nor could we have managed without the guidance and counsel of Beverly Loder, Tim Johnson, and Paula Tsurutani at the ABA. And finally, a special thanks to two of my colleagues at the McLane Law Firm, Ginny Dahlfred and Denise Penaskovic.

Arthur G. Greene
Editor

INTRODUCTION
Adapting to Change

Arthur G. Greene

Pervasive change affects every part of society and its institutions. Change has become the one constant for law firms. Hardly a week passes without the demise of a seemingly successful firm being announced. To defend against becoming another statistic in the failed firm obituaries, law firms must recognize and confront the phenomenon of change.

Success now depends on the firm's ability to respond to the market and to implement changes faster than its competition. Because lawyers tend to be set in their ways, affecting this change is no easy task.

Much can be learned by looking at the characteristics of firms that fail. Postmortem discussions often highlight the fact that such firms simply do not respond to the need to change. The lawyers may be stuck in their attitudes and their ways, and the firm leaders do not lead them away from the methods of practice that prevailed in the 1970s and 1980s. In contrast, firms that remain successful tend to have both strong leadership and a centralized governing structure that allows for a quick response to changes in the marketplace.

Lawyers who practiced in the old days—that is, the 1970s and early 1980s—find this trend to be unsettling. In earlier times, law firm stability was based on client loyalty and an abundance of good legal work. Both factors have changed. Competition for clients brought on by a constantly expanding population of lawyers has depressed the price most lawyers can charge for their services. Clients expect more for less, and they are quick to shop for a new firm. *Strengthening the firm* has become a real challenge for law firm leaders.

WHAT HAS CHANGED

The 1990s have brought a shift in the balance of power between lawyers and clients. Clients now control the relationship, and lawyers must react to the pressures of the marketplace. Successful practitioners must respond both effectively and quickly to the demands of clients. These demands may involve a client's need for more involvement in the planning and execution of a project, a change in the methods of practice, different staffing of a project, a requirement for more rapid technological advances, or simply better service at a lower cost.

Because of the intense competition among lawyers in private practice, clients are using their newfound power to force change. Most clients are not mean-spirited. They are operating in their own difficult marketplace and no longer have the luxury of maintaining relationships with law firms that do not respond to their needs. The global economy of the 1990s is putting U.S. corporations to the test. Can they bring efficiencies and cost control to their own products and compete in the international marketplace? Can they manage the faster pace and increased demands of business clients in their own battle for survival?

RECOGNIZING THE NEED FOR CHANGE

Many law firms face a variety of problems that can drive the firm into a downward spiral in which one problem leads to the next. Firms must identify their problems and recognize the significance of negative trends. Waiting too long to confront these problems increases the likelihood that the spiral will be irreversible.

The problems facing law firms fall into two broad groups: (1) those that are extrinsic to the law firm itself and (2) those that relate to the organization's internal management.

External Factors

The external factors may be briefly summarized as follows:

- **The Economy of the 1990s:** Clients are finding that they need to cut costs to compete in the 1990s. Business clients are more inclined to keep work in house or to manage and restrict the work performed by outside counsel. Consumer clients are more reluctant to seek legal advice and, if they do, may get their advice from non-lawyers or popularly priced firms. In any event, the amount of good legal work is contracting.
- **The Supply of Lawyers:** The number of lawyers entering the profession in recent years has greatly exceeded the ability of law firms to assimilate them. As a result, clients have a number of high-quality lawyers to consider and can shop for price. Technological advances have leveled the playing field and removed many of the advantages previously held by large firms. Unlike any time in the past, the client can dictate how much will be paid for a service. The client can limit the lawyer's role and can manage cost through the use of billing guidelines.

2

Internal Factors

The internal factors may be briefly summarized as follows:

- **Pressure on Lawyer Rates:** To compete in the current marketplace, many lawyers have had to quote lower rates or otherwise compromise their charges. They are often required to submit the lowest bid to acquire a project. Lawyers are being required to produce more for less.

- **Cost Cutting:** To produce work at lower rates, lawyers have had to cut back on their costs. In many cases this process has resulted in lawyers having to get by with less support. Pressures on the remaining staff increase and morale suffers. There is often an increase of tension in the firm, and it becomes a less desirable place to work.

- **Work Quality:** By taking on more work in an effort to reverse the trend, the quality of the firm's work product may suffer.

- **Associates:** Clients resist paying for associate work. Opportunities for on-the-job training will continue to decrease, and firms will have difficulty finding the time to initiate other means of training. Partnership decisions will be delayed. Associates will question whether to remain with the firm. Because of permanent staff lawyers and lateral hires, there will be fewer openings—but at what cost?

- **Partner Compensation:** There is an increasing need to reward the strong performers, regardless of age. Seniority alone can no longer be the basis of high compensation. An increased focus on a partner's "numbers" will cause a breakdown in teamwork, as each partner strives to be perceived as a strong performer. Firms must face up to a major adjustment in their compensation plans. As a result, partner relations may become strained.

- **Lack of Vision and Goals:** A firm in trouble will focus exclusively on short-term cash needs. Vision and goals will be ignored, assuming that they exist. The lack of a long-term plan will further exacerbate the existing problem.

- **Burnout:** Lawyer burnout will become prevalent and will lead to increasing inefficiency. It may afflict the firm's best lawyers. Some lawyers will consider leaving the profession.

- **Firm Income:** Firm income will be in decline. The lawyers will be working harder and making less. They will be told that the 1980s are gone and they must adjust their expectations. For some, the adjustment will be impossible.

- **Departures:** Partners will begin to leave for better opportunities. The best partners will go first. The partners the firm wants to unload will stay. All of this will cause associates to be concerned about the future of the firm. The best associates will go first. At some point, the firm can come down under its own weight. How many departures can a firm stand without failing? It depends—but each departure of a strong partner brings the firm closer to that line.

Unless the downward spiral is reversed, liquidation or significant restructuring is inevitable.

The key is to recognize the danger signs and do something about them. Once a firm recognizes those signs, it must muster the strength and the resolve to accept the need for change. The required change may be far-reaching. It may be uncomfortable. It may seem bold and risky. However, continuing business as usual may be creating a greater risk. The firm's survival may be at stake.

WHAT CHANGES MAY BE NECESSARY?

The changes being forced on law firms are client driven. They involve the need for attention to client objectives, better client communication, improved productivity, and legal bills that reflect the value added. While these practice management changes come under the category of client service, the ramifications spread to many internal issues, some of which may strike at the heart of the partnership relationship.

Strengthening Your Firm: Strategies for Success is designed to alert law firm leaders to the issues, both external and internal, that can challenge the firm and to provide the insight necessary to lead the firm successfully into the future. Some have used the term "revolution" to describe the magnitude of change that is being forced on law firms by clients. While the issues start with client service, they do not end there.

Improved Client Service at a Reasonable Cost

Lawyers are being forced to find innovative ways to meet their clients' demands for high-quality service at a reasonable cost. They know that if they fail to meet their clients' needs, some other lawyer will. They know that they must do a better job of understanding their clients' objectives and working with clients to develop a case or project plans. They need to communicate better with their clients and to find a way to meet clients' objectives for a fair price.

Increasingly, clients are the ones who decide how much they will pay. To meet the client demand for reduced cost, the lawyer may invest more time in a project than a client is willing to pay. Under those circumstances, the lawyer will have to write off some of the time, which will have an adverse effect on revenues. If the lawyer is unwilling or unable to perform the service for what the client deems to be a fair price, the client will find another lawyer who will.

As clients insist on a more competitive price, lawyers are faced with the need to produce a greater volume of legal work to meet revenue budgets. In addition to bringing in more work, lawyers must find a way to be more productive through delegation to legal assistants and better use of substantive computer systems. Further specialization will be essential as small boutique firms and small practice groups in large firms maximize efficiencies to enhance client service.

Technology

Investment in technology is an important tool to lawyers seeking to meet client demands for better service at a lower cost. Such investment may seem optional to some lawyers. However, it will only seem that way until the day a major client departs because it concludes that its lawyer is not keeping up with the times. Most sophisticated clients expect their lawyers to be at least as advanced as they are.

Many lawyers find it difficult to recover costs invested in technology. This is particularly true of lawyers who bill by the hour. In many respects the combination of lower fees and higher costs is making it difficult for lawyers to meet their income expectations.

Cost Control

Lawyers who have produced less revenue owing to client pressure on the cost of services have been forced to reduce their own costs. Consultants often urge firms to recognize that the solution to financial problems is to produce more revenue, not to decrease costs. While the theory may be sound, some firms have found improved revenue production impossible and have resorted to cost cutting to manage in difficult times. Certainly any firm that engaged in excessive spending during the 1980s must make adjustments to account for the fundamental changes resulting from a tough economy.

Downsizing

Cost cutting will produce only limited savings unless the firm tackles people costs through some type of downsizing. Typically secretaries are the first target, followed by administrative and other support staff. Great care must be taken to ensure that the firm does not reduce needed capacity. If there is an excess of legal talent, associates become the next casualty. Although most firms resist for a period of time, effective downsizing eventually involves one or more partners.

Accountability

It soon becomes apparent that partners must be more accountable to the firm as an institution, both with regard to revenue production and compliance with firm policies. As budgets become tighter, law firms discover that they can no longer afford to maintain unproductive partners. Partner evaluations have become the norm. Partner departures are not uncommon.

Compensation Systems

In difficult times, the law firm needs to use its compensation system as a management tool by undertaking to reward desired behavior and penalize unwanted behavior. The firm's largest producers must be adequately rewarded and they cannot be expected to carry unproductive partners. In fast-changing times, it may be necessary to reevaluate and adjust the compensation system. For example, the production of quality clients may be more important today than in years past. Increasingly, firms will look for ways to reward partners for teamwork. It is important that the compensation system be reexamined at least every five years to be certain that it continues to reflect the firm's needs.

Competition

Competition for the good work has become intense. Getting one's fair share of the legal work is no longer enough. Successful lawyers will be those who distinguish themselves in a way that results in their getting more than their fair share.

Marketing

Competition has brought many changes to the legal profession. The need to maintain a suitable portion of the legal business has caused most firms to work on distinguishing themselves in an effort to find a market niche. Marketing has become an effective and expensive way to develop and maintain the necessary client base. Lawyers who fail to recognize the importance of an appropriate level of marketing activity may find business shifting to others.

What Is the Alternative?

The need for change is resulting in a reengineering of law firms. It affects all aspects of the practice of law. It relates to how we get clients, how we work with them, how we manage their work, how we communicate with them, and how we bill them. Law firm leaders have the responsibility of helping the practicing lawyers identify the need for change and assisting them to implement that change. The alternative is to be "beat out" by the competition.

WHAT DOES CHANGE HAVE TO DO WITH A BOOK ON PARTNERSHIPS?

The test for survival in these times is whether the law firm can adapt to change. The firm's success will depend on both its governing structure and the leadership abilities of those in control.

Historically, law firms have been slow to change. Management structures have been too democratic. Lawyers are not trained in management and they try to manage in their spare time. They tend to be "take charge" people who are convinced that their view is the only correct one. Unfortunately, changes do not get made in the face of controversy, and traditional consensus building can be too slow.

Those law firms able to implement the changes necessary to respond to their clients' demands will survive and thrive. In most cases, those firms have moved away from democracy to a more centralized management structure. In addition, most of those firms have good managers and effective leaders who inspire the confidence of the partners. Nothing less is likely to succeed in these times.

This volume focuses on partnership issues that are important to the law firm that needs to remain strong and healthy. There are three important steps:

1. Understand the challenges faced by the firm and the wide range of changes that are necessary to compete successfully.
2. Next, evaluate how the firm's governing structure will affect its ability to respond to those challenges. If it is too cumbersome to allow the firm to make the changes necessary to remain competitive, the underlying structure may require study and change.
3. Finally, the law firm must recognize that good management is not enough. Every firm needs an effective leader who can communicate a vision and bring necessary changes to the firm in a timely manner.

There will be winners and losers in the years ahead. The successful firms will be those able to remain competitive by adopting changes required by the environment in which they operate. This economic Darwinism may be frightening to all practitioners, and disastrous to some, but for those who are willing to embrace change and to adapt to the demands of the marketplace, it may signal new opportunities for growth and success in the practice of law.

CHAPTER I
Partnership Challenges

Gerry Malone

Law firm life was fairly simple twenty years ago. Firms worked for loyal clients, and individual lawyers were not expected to generate their own client base. If the lawyers did good work, they became partners in the firm after a few years. If the firm did good work, more work followed naturally. Not much attention was paid to competition, to the economics of the practice, or to internal management. The founding father or senior partner was the managing partner. In large firms, the senior partner in each practice area was the department head; in small firms, each lawyer managed his or her own practice. Management was a laissez faire function of firm life.

Why is running a law firm so much more difficult today? The short answer is *competition*. Competition's impact on the profession over the past twenty years has stunned many lawyers. Little has been left unchanged—the practice, the clients, the demographics, the economics, the market, law firm management, and the meaning of partnership. Simply put, life in a law firm is more complicated than it formerly was. Consider, for example, the following factors:

- The increased competition. The number of lawyers has grown faster than the available work necessary to keep those lawyers productive. That, along with the growing emphasis on marketing, has meant keen competition for all available business.
- The focus on the business aspects of the practice. Years ago, for all practical purposes, partnership was automatic. Many still cling to this tradition but are under pressure to adopt a different approach to partnership—one in which partners must be good business people and marketers as well as good lawyers. Well-managed firms now pay significant attention to business management principles to maximize and maintain an economic return on their practice.
- The shift to a buyer's market. Gone are the days of the loyal or institutional client that is locked into one firm. Clients, both corporate and individual, are much more sophisticated purchasers of legal services. They demand a high level of legal work and a high level of service, while clamoring for

reduced legal expenses. When clients' demands are not met, there is a wealth of lawyers waiting in the wings, and clients are well aware of this.

- The diversity in law firms. In years past, most partners in law firms went to the same schools or types of schools, moved in the same social circles, and held the same political and business views. Many firms now realize the need to reflect their client base and are pushing to diversify. Diversification has many advantages, but it is more challenging to manage and direct diverse groups.

- Decreased partner and firm loyalty. It used to be that "once a partner, always a partner" was the one thing lawyers could count on. Today, however, it is not unusual for firms to ask partners to leave, and downsizing, or "rightsizing," is the order of the day. Add to this the fact that partners themselves have become extremely mobile, often moving to the firm that will pay them the most for their book of business, or to the firm that best reflects their priorities and goals.

How these changes affect a firm will depend on its ability to adapt, but it is fairly certain that most firms in the next ten years will face many of the same challenges. Strong leadership, a willingness to adapt, and effective management will be key ingredients to success.

In addition to issues discussed in other chapters of this book, some of the most critical challenges facing law firms in the next ten years are discussed in this chapter, along with recommendations for dealing with those challenges. These include the following:

- Creating a culture that provides both a motivating work environment and a competitive edge in the marketplace
- Communicating effectively with all firm members about issues that are most important to each group
- Achieving an appropriate balance between partner accountability and partner autonomy
- Maintaining good partner relationships
- Dealing with problem partners
- Rightsizing, or maintaining a cost-effective and competitive work force
- Planning
- Diversifying and creating a culture in which all can be comfortable
- Transitioning clients to the next generation
- Responding to strong leadership and transitioning leadership to the next generation

FIRM CULTURE

A firm's culture forms the foundation for the firm's work environment. Firm culture is most easily defined by the relationships between the partners and the relationships between the firm and its employees. It determines, among other things, the following:

- Whether the firm is an institution that effectively uses a team approach or is simply a group of lawyers sharing space and overhead to advance individual goals
- The extent to which clients are seen as *firm* clients
- The extent to which the partners share common values, such as work ethics, quality of work, and service to clients
- The level of autonomy individual lawyers have and the extent to which they are accountable to the firm
- The way partners are compensated and the value placed on various contributions made by the partners
- The way the firm is governed and the extent to which partners are involved in day-to-day operations
- The way associates are trained, supervised, and, ultimately, made partners.
- Whether the firm's focus is on short-term profitability or long-term security and stability

A culture that promotes a *firm first* attitude can be a firm's greatest strength. When people at all levels in the firm think in terms of what is best for the firm—an institutional approach—the firm becomes the central focus and provides a more stable environment.

TECHNIQUES FOR CREATING AN INSTITUTIONAL CULTURE

In today's legal environment, developing a firm culture that promotes the firm and a work environment that satisfies most people professionally and economically is no easy task. Nevertheless, it can be done.

Partners set the tone for creating the culture the firm wishes to achieve. As the firm goes through various cycles in its evolution, its culture may evolve, either because of economic necessity or because of a change in leadership.

Historically, a firm's culture was created through a process guided by the founders. In a new firm, the partners can define the culture they want to achieve by setting goals and defining specific strategies for accomplishing those goals. Every lawyer comes to a firm with his or her own set of biases and experiences that influence the decision-making process and life at the firm. Still, by discussing shared values and agreeing that these values will be preserved as the firm defines its strategy for moving forward, the partners can ensure that they are creating the kind of culture they want.

The issues discussed in the remainder of this chapter all affect the firm's culture, either in a positive or a negative way. It is incumbent on the firm's leadership to keep the partners focused on the importance of being an institutional firm.

COMMUNICATION

Ask partners, associates, paralegals, or support staff to identify their firm's weaknesses, and they will almost always list a lack of communication. One group may perceive a problem to be more troublesome than another group does, or for a different reason, but on the whole, people who work in law firms today want more information about issues that affect them. The underlying lesson, however, is that complaints about the lack of communication are often symptoms of deeper problems.

Partners

Partners typically point to communication problems when the firm is experiencing strategic or financial problems. If partners in the firm are complaining about a lack of communication, it is likely because of one or more of the following reasons:

- Partners feel that the firm is without direction. Neither they nor the firm have specific goals, and partners may feel that they are working at cross-purposes.
- Some partners are unhappy with the performance of one or more other partners but are unwilling to or incapable of discussing the problem with the partner or partners involved.
- The firm is financially strained and partners want more information, (i.e., a greater comfort level) that will make them feel more secure about the firm's future.
- Management does not have a high priority within the firm—the perception is that it is not rewarded in compensation, or partners are more concerned about autonomy than having a well-managed firm. Thus, those in management positions do not devote much time to it. As a result, no one spends much time talking about management issues. Decisions get made without adequate consideration or without enough consensus building, or decisions don't get made at all until issues reach crisis proportions.
- The firm has recently undergone a change from management by democracy to management by a smaller group or a single person. Since partners have been accustomed to being involved in the most minor decisions, they feel that they must still be kept informed about such decisions. While centralized management is usually a more efficient form of governance, it also requires a higher level of communication.
- Partners do not often work on client matters together, and they do not socialize. If the partners do not meet as professionals, don't hold occasional meetings or retreats, or don't socialize, they don't get to know each other well enough to trust that all partners want the same things out of the practice of law and their firm.

Associates

Ask young lawyers to expand on their sense of lack of communication, and—regardless of firm size—they most often cite the following types of issues:

- The firm lacks direction. Associates do not know the firm's goals or even if there are goals. The seniors in law firms don't realize that most young people today are goal oriented and less willing than the older generation was to trust their future to something simply because others say that "it has always worked."

- The partners don't agree on firm direction. This results in mixed messages to associates about what they can expect from the firm in the future.

- The firm does not have an associate development program for young lawyers. Training is catch-as-catch-can at best or completely nonexistent. Sink-or-swim training means that young lawyers are often thrown considerable responsibility without much supervision or meaningful evaluation. This is especially true in small firms.

- Associates perceive a high level of turnover among their group, but they see no concerted effort by the partners to address the problem and no communication or warning signs about those who are leaving.

- The partners provide little guidance to associates about how to be successful as lawyers and as businesspeople, despite the fact that associates want to know what they must do to become partners. During tough economic times firms often raise the standards for partnership admissions but then fail to define those standards in any meaningful way.

Legal Assistants

Despite their growing presence in the profession over the past twenty years, legal assistants in many firms have not yet been effectively integrated into the practice. Legal assistants often point to the same types of communication issues that associates do, but some communication issues are unique to legal assistants.

- As with partners and associates, legal assistants can sense a lack of firm direction or specified goals. They often assume that there are goals but that the partners don't feel the legal assistants are important enough to be included in a discussion of those goals.

- Legal assistants often feel that they are not treated as professionals. They often blame the partners for not effectively educating clients, young lawyers, and support staff about legal assistants' professional status and role in the firm. The partners send subtle messages that legal assistants are not important members of the legal services delivery team, often giving the impression they are extensions of the support staff.

- A major problem for many legal assistants is the firm's failure to define the expectations it has of legal assistants. There is a vague message that legal assistants are expected to bill a certain number of hours, but there is no corresponding plan to ensure that the work is available or that the hours are billed. Closely related to the firm's failure to provide information about expectations is its failure to provide legal assistants with meaningful evaluations.

- As with associates, legal assistants often feel there is a lack of communication regarding substantive legal matters. Legal assistants are given assignments with only vague instructions and little ongoing supervision or direction. It is not unusual for a legal assistant to work throughout the weekend on a trial set for Monday only to learn on Monday that the case was settled on Friday.

Support Staff

Law firm partners do not always understand that support staff have many of the same needs as legal staff. For support staff, the problem is sometimes the *type* of communication as well as the fact that there is insufficient communication.

- In some firms support staff are referred to as "non-lawyer staff" or, worse yet, "nonprofessional staff." This negative reference to status is unique to the legal profession, and clients often notice it. Support staff in most law firms describe themselves as professional, and they want the partners to view them as making a valuable contribution to the firm's success.

- Support staff want to feel that they are working toward firm goals. They too suffer from a lack of communication about firm strategy and direction. In one large firm in the Southwest, for example, the firm makes it clear that one of its goals is to be more responsive to clients than is any other firm with which the client works. The message being communicated to staff is clear: Do what it takes to get the job done. They do, and they are proud of their contribution.

- In firms that have no office manager or administrator, or have an administrator without authority, the staff often complain about the lack of communication. There is no "official" system for communicating policy, procedures, expectations, or performance standards. If each individual lawyer is responsible for communicating such, each staff person will receive a different message. The result is a perception that "there are no rules" or that "the rules don't apply equally to everyone."

Communication problems can and do exist in firms of all sizes. As a firm grows, the problems may become more acute, especially if there were serious communication problems when the firm was smaller.

TECHNIQUES FOR COMMUNICATING EFFECTIVELY

An effective communication process is an evolutionary one in any law firm. As a firm's needs change over time, communication systems and processes need to change to accommodate those needs. In addition, needs will vary from time to time. For example, a firm in crisis requires more communication than one in which everything is working smoothly.

It is important for those in leadership positions to be aware of changing communication needs at any given time. Leaders must also be willing to devote time to provide the level of communication necessary to ensure that both legal and support staff understand the firm's goals and priorities, what is expected of them, and how they fit into the firm's overall plan. Clearly, all of this is easier said than done.

It is easy to say that the only way to improve communication is by doing it. Finding the time as well as the appropriate techniques is not always so easy. Except in very small firms where all communication responsibilities rest with a managing partner (or the sole proprietor), communication responsibilities are usually spread among many people. Many firms have an office manager or administrator who is responsible for communication with support staff. In some firms a management or executive committee shares communication responsibilities, or a partner may have specific responsibilities for a given function, such as associate management.

An effective communications network must begin with the partners. An effective governance structure, which all partners buy into, should assign responsibility for communication at all levels. Even in small firms, identifying and assigning specific responsibilities for communication helps avoid confusion and mixed signals. Once roles are defined, it is important to allow those given the responsibility to handle the communications. The individual partners should agree and commit to the following:

- They will keep partnership matters confidential. Although some partners, under the guise of being honest and open, discuss issues with everyone, in most instances the result is divisive. Unfortunately, most firms pay only lip service to the need for confidentiality and are unwilling to deal with those partners who routinely violate that trust.
- Once a partnership vote is taken on an issue and a decision is made, they will not continue to discuss the issue, especially outside of partnership meetings, for the same reasons

just discussed. It is important for the partners not to undermine each other.

- They will not interfere with the agreed-on processes. If their assigned staff ask policy questions of them, they will refer staff to the person assigned responsibility for that particular issue.

Once the tone is set at the partnership level, it becomes easier to implement specific communication processes to enhance harmony at all levels.

Strategic Goals and Firm Direction

Setting strategic goals and firm direction and communicating those to everyone in the firm is an effective way to build a cohesive firm. Since strategic planning is a continuous, never-ending process, communication about goals should become a "standard" issue to be discussed with all firm members. The best approach is to think of communication of goals as an integral part of the firm's operations.

Retreats

It is almost impossible for a law firm to address strategic planning effectively at the weekly or monthly partnership meetings, no matter how small the firm. This generally results in strategic business matters continually being moved to the back burner, since the pressure of daily workloads requires partners to expend most of their energy producing legal services within specified deadlines. Day-to-day operational issues are more easily handled at regularly scheduled meetings of the management group or, to a lesser extent, of the partnership. From a communications and strategic standpoint, however, an annual retreat is perhaps the best technique a law firm can use. Retreats should focus on long-range and strategic issues rather than on operational ones. The partners should discuss and reach consensus on issues that involve the firm's growth, client service, practice management, business development, future practices, partner relationships, and issues of that nature.

Some firms include associates for some retreats or agenda items. For example, if the retreat focus is social, all lawyers may be invited. While social retreats have great value in many situations (e.g., immediately following a merger or a large group joining the firm), the most effective retreats tend to be those that deal with strategic issues, particularly practice integration.

Traditionally, firm retreats have included all partners working their way through a planned agenda. This approach is still effective for small firms. In larger firms, however, this approach is declining in use as firms discover the benefits of smaller, more highly focused planning sessions. Depending on the firm's size, the retreat format may be planned to have designated groups working on a specific issue, such as in the following examples:

- A firm engaged in a strategic planning process might have groups of four to six partners working on a given issue. One group might address expansion opportunities, another a client targeting strategy, and another a plan for improved client service. The groups would report at some point in the meeting, and each issue would be discussed and consensus reached.

- A firm interested in alternative pricing might form work groups by practice area, with each group using an actual client matter (already concluded and billed) to arrive at other ways the matter might have been priced.

- In large and medium-sized firms, leadership groups often use a mini-retreat setting to engage in strategic planning for the firm. The focus of a management retreat may be strategic or tactical planning.

- Departmental or practice group retreats are becoming very common and are among the most effective planning approaches. Once the practice groups or departments hold their retreats, the management group may retreat to refine and improve those plans.

Simply holding the retreat, however, is not enough. There must be follow-through. The group should set specific goals, someone should be assigned responsibility for accomplishing the goals within specified time periods, and the managing partner (or a designated member of the management group) should ensure that it happens. The partners who accept responsibilities of this type should be held accountable (through compensation) for fulfilling such commitments.

Partnership Meetings

Formats for partnership meetings vary considerably, depending on firm size, governance structure, and culture. Ideally, even in small firms, partnership meetings are used to deal with substantive issues as much as possible, leaving administrative details to specified lawyers or an administrator. Partnership meetings should be used to accomplish the following:

- Make decisions on important issues. If the firm has a managing partner or a designated management group, all discussion of such issues should be accompanied by that person's or group's recommendations, along with the reasons for those recommendations.
- Discuss significant new work as well as marketing opportunities for additional work. These discussions often lead to ideas on how to take the best advantage of such opportunities.

- Bring the partners up to date on the state of the firm. The managing partner (or other appropriate person) should give a report on the "state of the firm," commenting on things such as financial performance, major firm or client projects currently underway, and major projects anticipated for the future.
- Give the partners a *brief* administrative report. This reporting (by the administrator, if the firm has one) should not be a forum for rehashing administrative decisions but merely for advising partners of major administrative decisions that have been made or administrative projects that are underway.
- Encourage some social interchange among the partners, either before or after the meeting.

To be most productive, partnership meetings should be held at a regularly scheduled time and place. Annually the managing partner or administrator should distribute a calendar of meetings to all partners so that they can hold the dates open, if possible. In addition, the managing partner should implement a process that allows partners to place issues on the agenda for discussion. (Such issues should be limited to those that are reserved to the partners for decision.) Partners would have a designated time period before the meeting to place items on the agenda. The agenda would be distributed to all partners before the meeting. Minutes of meetings would either be distributed to partners following the meeting or available for reading in the office of the managing partner or other designated partner.

Operational or Day-to-Day Communications

Primary responsibility for communication in any law firm rests with the managing partner, the designated member of the management group, or the de facto firm leader as well as with the office manager or administrator, if one exists. For purposes of this discussion, we use the terms "managing partner" and "administrator."

The Managing Partner's Role in Communications

Communication is one of the most important responsibilities of the managing partner. When partners in a law firm delegate management responsibilities to a single person (or a small group), they are demonstrating their trust in that individual to keep them informed of, and to ask for their input on, important issues. Regardless of the level of authority for decision making, the managing partner cannot make those decisions in a vacuum. Building consensus for decisions is critical. Thus, the managing partner should do the following:

- "Walk the halls" regularly and talk with both lawyers and staff, making it a point to have regular one-on-one conversations with every lawyer in the firm. These conversations provide a forum for learning individual's priorities and opinions about major firm issues and for building consensus. Many managing partners feel that if they announce an open door policy, everything will take care of itself. However, an open door policy is not a substitute for walking the halls because people don't always recognize problems on their own. Moreover, waiting for people to bring their problems to the managing partner generally means that the managing partner reacts to problems rather than prevents them.

- Visit lawyers personally to follow up on questions or issues they have asked be addressed or to discuss the outcome of a decision that affects the lawyer personally.
- Meet annually with every person who has management responsibilities of any kind to help them set goals and priorities for the coming year.
- Meet annually with each of the firm's top twenty clients to solicit input about the performance of the firm and its lawyers.
- Ensure that associates and legal assistants are being given adequate communication and direction about substantive work as well as administrative matters that affect them.
- Be accessible to lawyers and to the firm administrator.
- Stay in touch with the lawyers through voice mail or memos, especially between partnership and other "formal" meetings.

The Administrator's Role in Communications

Communication is also one of the most important responsibilities of the administrator. In addition to helping the managing partner perform his or her responsibilities, the administrator must also ensure that staff members receive the level of communication they need to be most productive. This means ensuring that staff understand the following:

- General firm policies that affect them, such as medical and retirement benefits, the firm's compensation plan, firm holidays, administrative and accounting processes, and where to go for help
- Their individual roles in the firm, including their job responsibilities, what the firm expects of them, and how they will be evaluated for job performance
- Annual evaluations providing feedback on job performance and setting professional development goals
- Available support in achieving professional development goals
- Changes that affect staff
- Firm goals, with particular attention to those that affect staff directly

- Administrative issues of concern or interest to the staff
- Ways to improve workflow and efficiency
- Important events in the life of the firm

Social Gatherings

The purpose of social gatherings is simply to give firm members the opportunity to know each other. If the firm has partners who came in laterally, such social interaction is even more important. Opportunities for social interaction are usually easiest at the partner level. Partnership meetings and retreats, for example, can easily be planned to include specified social time.

Some small firms have a weekly lawyers' luncheon, the sole purpose of which is to provide a social forum for the lawyers. (Legal assistants may periodically be invited to the luncheon as well.) The luncheon is held at a regular time and place, and lawyers who are available attend. To work effectively, *partners must* attend. Otherwise, the event deteriorates into an "associates' lunch," although the primary value is to allow partners and associates to get to know each other.

It is usually beneficial to have at least one annual firm function that all firm members attend (sometimes with spouses or significant others). The primary value of such an event is to demonstrate to staff that the firm views them as important members of the services delivery team. Most often these events are in the form of an annual holiday party or summer picnic. For such events to accomplish their purpose, partners must attend.

In addition, many firms also have social get-togethers to celebrate the following:

- Birthdays of lawyers, legal assistants, and staff
- The arrival of a new lawyer, legal assistant, or staff member
- A retirement after a long tenure at the firm
- A major renovation of some type (e.g., the library)
- Any significant event in the life of the firm (e.g., winning a major case, completing a substantial transaction, gaining an important new client)

These types of events not only make the honored people feel important but also enhance camaraderie throughout the firm.

ACCOUNTABILITY

One of the significant challenges of life in a partnership is striking the appropriate balance between lawyer autonomy and accountability. Lawyer autonomy dates back to the beginning of the profession. Even as lawyers formed partnerships, the individual lawyers held sacred each lawyer's right to total autonomy, even to the detriment of others in the firm. This attitude was prevalent as recently as ten years ago, especially in small and medium-sized firms. While it is not as pervasive today, the attitude still exists.

Although many lawyers still cling to personal autonomy, most realize that they also owe a measure of accountability to others in the firm—the big question is how much. There is no easy answer to this question, and each firm must find the appropriate balance for itself. Most firms bite the bullet when it becomes obvious that total autonomy comes at too high a price. Perhaps partner incomes decline because too many partners refuse to pay attention to how their behavior affects firm profitability. Maybe the firm experiences a rash of malpractice claims that not only diminish the bottom line but result in unfavorable publicity and the loss of clients. For example, consider partners who do the following:

- Don't turn in their time sheets when due. As a result, bills cannot go out on time, some of the time is never recovered, and the profitability of the work is diminished.
- Don't follow realistic work intake guidelines to ensure that the client will pay and the work is appropriate for the firm.
- Are a malpractice risk to the firm, either because they are not good lawyers, don't pay enough attention to quality control, practice beyond their level of competence, or don't do a good job communicating with clients.
- Pay little attention to billing and collection guidelines. They "don't have time to bill" or to pressure clients on past due accounts receivable. They protect deadbeat clients to the detriment of their fellow partners.
- Don't specialize to the extent they should. They believe they can be all things to all clients, regardless of what their fellow partners believe.
- Don't treat other partners' client work with the same degree of care with which they treat their "own" client work.
- Make no effort to help train young lawyers or to help make them profitable.
- Make no effort to participate in firmwide marketing efforts.
- Pay little attention to firm management policies and guidelines.
- Put their own needs above those of the other partners. For example, they feel they have the right to spend money any way they choose.
- Show no respect for other professionals in the firm, such as for their ideas, values, gender, ethnic background, or age.

At some point in their growth curve, most firms realize that client service would improve along with firm profitability if partners were willing to be more accountable. Most institutional firms, as the legal industry matures, develop a culture that eventually brings them to an appropriate balance. Some firms don't balance out over time and suddenly find themselves in crisis situations, having to make major changes over a short time just to survive. When accountability must be implemented overnight, the transition is difficult at best. If the transition must include a different management team or if the firm lacks strong leadership, the firm is at risk. Outside assistance may be needed to get the firm back on track.

A firm retreat is an excellent forum for addressing accountability—it is a strategic planning issue because the implementation of any goals the firm sets will be affected by the level of accountability required of those responsible. For example, if the goal is to improve firm profitability, the plan will no doubt include numerous action steps needed to reach the profitability goal. Those might consist of (1) all partners working at a minimum level beyond the current levels, (2) implementing work acceptance guidelines, (3) implementing firm-controlled billing and collection guidelines, and (4) ensuring that associates and legal assistants are productive. It is easy to see that if partners are not accountable for their roles in carrying out the supporting activities, it is unlikely that the firm will ever meet the goal.

Owing to the immense potential liability facing law firms today, the current trend is to focus more on accountability than on autonomy, and those unwilling to be accountable are asked to leave. Many firms have learned the hard way that it is impossible to be successful without requiring accountability.

TECHNIQUES FOR ENCOURAGING ACCOUNTABILITY

Even if the partners agree that accountability is a vital ingredient in a successful law firm, integrating that concept into the firm's culture can still be difficult. It takes time, commitment, and leadership, and, most importantly, the willingness and the mechanism (i.e., partner compensation) to enforce accountability.

Firm Culture

The ideal way to achieve accountability is through the firm's culture. In firms where the concept of accountability has been demonstrated at the top, accountability has become a way of life. A firm need not impose heavy-handed oversight of the fundamental aspects of each lawyer's practice. However, the firm does need to maintain and enforce high standards of performance. Certainly in a successful law firm, partners are encouraged to be innovative and creative in client service and practice development, but that creativity must be exercised within reasonable bounds. Partners need to understand that accountability is simply a business principle that must be applied to ensure firm success.

Personal Goal Setting

Many firms are now using personal goal-setting plans both to expedite implementation of strategic planning and to put teeth into their accountability standards. This approach calls for an annual plan from each partner (usually approved by firm management) concerning the following:

- Billable hours and collections goals
- Nonbillable contributions, customized to the individual's management and marketing responsibilities, often to implement certain aspects of the firm's strategic plan
- Business development goals, including expansion of existing clients, cross-marketing, new business development, and targeted prospective clients
- Practice management goals, including client service quality, delegation of clients and work, productivity of associates and legal assistants working with the partner, and transitioning clients to others
- CLE, professional, and civic activities, including specific CLE needs and involvement in professional and civic organizations (e.g., writing, speaking, holding office)
- Plans to overcome unique individual weaknesses

Personal game plans help to enhance accountability, and they also serve as a basis for evaluation in subjective compensation determinations. Most successful firms rely on their compensation system as both a carrot and a stick. By penalizing partners who do not live up to their responsibilities, a firm can slowly change its culture so that lack of adherence to firm policies is the exception rather than the rule.

Evaluation

As the idea of accountability begins to take root in many firms, evaluating accountability becomes a part of the compensation process. It is difficult, however, to build accountability into a system that is based solely on objective data. In a subjective system, the kinds of criteria that might be evaluated include partners' level of cooperativeness in areas that affect profitability and client service but may not be readily apparent from objective data. Here are examples of such areas.

- Turning in time sheets, billing promptly, and cooperating in collections
- Training and supervising associates and legal assistants
- Delegating work, when appropriate, to other partners and associates
- Motivating and encouraging members of the team
- Participating in cross-marketing activities and transitioning clients
- Providing excellent legal work and quality services to all clients (and note that more and more firms are beginning to solicit client feedback, not only for quality control purposes but for improving client service and relations and for strategic planning purposes)

- Doing work at a level commensurate with one's experience and expertise

In some firms this evaluation is the responsibility of a management group or a compensation committee alone, while in other firms partners are asked to evaluate their fellow partners. In larger firms and in those with formalized practice management structures, practice leaders usually evaluate the accountability standards of those in their supervisory realm. Some firms have partners complete an evaluation form on the other partners' performance, with accountability standards being among the criteria. Most firms with subjective compensation systems use a process of partner interviews to elicit comprehensive feedback about partner performance.

Peer Review

For the most part, in today's legal profession peer review means quality assurance, that is, improving legal services to clients through a process of evaluation by peers or colleagues. This means that the quality of the lawyer's substantive work must be reviewed. Such evaluation can be problematic. Confidentiality of client work is the reason most often given, but if you read between the lines, lawyer nervousness about what a review of their work will mean to them is the real problem. Firms that have had the confidence to launch peer review programs have found clients cooperative.

There are definite advantages to a peer review system.

- It identifies serious quality control and substandard legal performance. This is particularly important because in some situations partners may be held liable for the acts of other partners of which they should have been aware. Also, partners are responsible for the quality of the work they delegate to associates.
- It improves the overall quality of a firm's work product, its delivery of legal services, and its profitability.
- It improves the supervision and training of young lawyers.
- It promotes continuing professional development.
- It enhances partner accountability.

Lawyers who resist the process take another view.

- It would take too much time and become a costly procedure.
- Documents generated during the process could be harmful in the event of claims (i.e., they could be discoverable).
- It could constitute expensive "overlawyering," the expense of which cannot and should not be passed on to the client.
- It is an intrusion on a lawyer's freedom to practice.
- It may be a violation of due process.
- Though designed to ensure quality work, it might be misinterpreted and misused during the partner compensation process.
- There could be a hidden agenda that could turn into a "witch hunt."

24

Most of these concerns, however, have little merit. Interestingly, experience shows a high correlation between the partners who raise these objectives and the incidence of problems.

The process itself varies from one in which firm lawyers review the files of other firm lawyers to one in which two law firms review each other's files (with client consent). At one end of the spectrum is a "cold" study and vigorous substantive evaluation of materials in conjunction with an extensive interview of the lawyer. At the other end is a passive system consisting of monitored adherence to a recommended checklist. The lawyer being reviewed merely assures the reviewing lawyer that certain steps have been followed.

Most firms define peer review in terms of partner evaluation for compensation purposes. Not many have carried the concept beyond a general, subjective evaluation of how partners perceive each other's performance. In a few firms associates evaluate partners as well, and this evaluation is used in the compensation process. Some firms have expanded the process to include an internal review of work product for adherence to quality standards. Very few have extended the process to a vigorous substantive evaluation of documents and related materials in conjunction with quality control standards and client and lawyer interviews.

There are ways that firm leaders may overcome arguments against peer review.

- Advocate what should get reviewed and how it gets reviewed.
- Keep this evaluation out of the direct compensation process, with the exception that the result might be considered as one fact. Don't do this evaluation at the same time as compensation evaluations.
- Be selective about what gets reviewed and when. Look at the most critical aspects of the work being done.
- Involve working groups of partners to identify critical areas of their practices that should be reviewed.
- Rather than starting with a substantive review of the work, begin by implementing a "technical standards review" of the work.

Even with these techniques, communication plays a major role in achieving acceptable levels of accountability. Once a firm sets guidelines for accountability, the firm's management person or group should notify and assist partners who have failed to measure up. If a problem is discussed and addressed as soon as it arises, it can often be resolved before it becomes a major, disruptive issue.

SPECIALIZATION

Consumers expect specialists in every walk of life, and legal services are no different. Few would argue that the current trend toward specialization will not continue. Specialization will be a key to differentiation in the marketplace. Differentiation will become more important as competition increases and clients become even more demanding. After all, how can a lawyer market himself or herself as a general practitioner? Marketing experts will say it is impossible, and clients uniformly say it is undesirable.

Still, many lawyers in small and medium-sized firms have fairly general practices, and some are hesitant to give up that flexibility. This produces a number of problems for the law firm.

- Marketing is much more difficult because the firm has no particular expertise, be it practice area or industry focus, that differentiates it from any other small general practice firm. As a result, partners complain that their marketing efforts are of little effectiveness, the client base stagnates, and firm profits drop.
- Since all partners are working on anything and everything, the efficiency and productivity resulting from comprehensive knowledge of a practice area are lost. In a firm in which most lawyers are in general practice, there is likely to be a great deal of wheel spinning and inadequate development of substantive systems. The reason is that it is everybody's job but nobody's job.
- Clients are more likely to complain about the bills because a project cost more than they expected. Bills are adjusted to keep clients happy, but profits drop.
- The risk of malpractice problems increases because the lawyers doing the work simply do not have the expertise needed to do the job. They may be hesitant to ask for help.
- Lawyers in the firm compete for the available work. This is especially true if the firm's compensation system rewards hours. This scenario opens the door for partner relationship problems.
- Training is much more difficult. Associates who work with generalists tend to be generalists as well. Since the law is so much more complex today, this is a severe problem. On the whole, associates who work as generalists do not progress as rapidly as lawyers who are specialized. This does not mean that associates should not receive broad-based training. They should. What it does mean is that they may not receive sufficient exposure in any one practice area to be proficient.

TECHNIQUES FOR INCREASING SPECIALIZATION

Once the partners agree that they need to increase their expertise in specific areas, it takes a lot of work to get there. Accordingly, the firm must develop a plan outlining the following:

- The specialties that each lawyer will pursue. In most firms it is not unusual for a lawyer to pursue more than one specialty. To the extent possible, a lawyer's focus should be limited to two practice areas and should never exceed three.

Otherwise, it will be impossible for the lawyer to call himself or herself a specialist. In addition, as part of their annual planning process, the partners should discuss which of their practice areas offer the greatest opportunities for business development. Then, partners should agree on which of them will concentrate on which areas. Associates should have the opportunity for input on the practice specialties they will pursue.

- The way work will be assigned. Once the firm decides which lawyers will do what types of work, the partners should agree that, whenever possible, that type of work will be funneled to the designated partner or partners. Even though client relationships and client demands will not always permit the work to be assigned as the firm would prefer, if the partners are diligent, they can reach their goal.

- Additional training needs. Some of the designated lawyers may need outside CLE to boost their substantive knowledge. CLE participation should revolve around these needs.

- Certification. As more state bar associations embrace the notion of certification, lawyers who specialize in designated practice areas will want to become certified. The firm should decide who should seek certification and in which areas.

- Compensation during transition. If the firm's compensation system is such that it will penalize partners for delegating certain types of work to other partners and associates, the firm's efforts at increasing specialization will not succeed. In fact, partners who are willing to sacrifice their own work (and hours) for the benefit of a specialization plan should be "made whole" in the firm's compensation arrangement.

- Time frames. This is not a transition that will happen overnight. On the contrary, the process can take several years. It is critical that all partners recognize that it will take time to accomplish the goal. The partners must be patient.

As the firm begins to see results, it should find ways to market these specialties. Results from marketing efforts may take time as well, so the entire process should be viewed as a long-term project, but one that promises significant rewards in the firm's future.

PARTNER RELATIONSHIPS

It is not unusual to find the personal relationships among the partners threatening the very survival of the firm. Relationships can become so strained that partners spend more time pointing fingers, arguing, and backbiting than they do worrying about what their competition may be doing to the firm and its client base.

Such problems exist in firms of all sizes and, interestingly, often in economically successful firms. Just as the dynamics of the marketplace have changed the way lawyers practice, those same dynamics have altered the meaning of partnership and the way the partners relate to each other. Some of the changes are a result of economic realities, while others are a result of altered attitudes and values. Recognizing the change is one thing; learning to live with it is quite another. Consider these typical scenarios that result in divisiveness, loss of trust, and sometimes open warfare among partners.

- One group of partners works extremely hard, perhaps averaging 2,400 billable hours per partner for the year. Another group averages about 1,700 hours. The harder-working group wants to maximize its income. The other group is more interested in what it sees as a reasonable quality of life.
- A few partners are extremely aggressive in their marketing and feel that all partners must take a similar approach if the firm is to thrive. Some of their partners understand the necessity of marketing but are not as aggressive.
- A few partners are underproductive because their practice expertise is obsolete. These partners are insecure about their futures and resentful that their many years of hard work and loyalty to the firm mean nothing. Some of their partners may resent having to help "support" partners who, they feel, are not carrying their weight, while others believe the firm must support all partners.
- The firm does work in a practice area where the profit margin is narrower than for other practice areas. Some partners want to eliminate the low-profit practice area. Others insist that this practice area is vital to providing the service some of the firm's important clients need or in training young lawyers.

These scenarios are symptoms of a much bigger problem—the partners are not headed in the same direction. As a result, tensions develop and relationships are damaged. These examples illustrate three major points about the partners in these firms.

1. They have different personal goals.
2. They have different expectations from the practice of law and from partnership in a firm.
3. They have different philosophic approaches to the practice.

As discussed previously, poor communication is a common weakness in firms experiencing partner problems. Communication is not as good as it should be because the partners are hesitant to talk to each other about sensitive issues. This hesitancy may be left over from the days when partners had total autonomy. Regardless, the problems become exacerbated because, instead of talking to each other about a problem, partners complain to other partners or, worse, to associates, legal assistants, or staff.

TECHNIQUES FOR IMPROVING PARTNER RELATIONSHIPS

The solutions—and there are no easy ones—lie in attacking the problem, not the symptoms. Each firm's values and its partners' personalities play a major role. Firm leaders are fundamental in helping the group find a common ground. In fact, they can often mandate what must be done to overcome the problem. Too often, however, no one has the inclination or leadership skills to help partners work through these difficulties. As a result, the partners often ignore the situation, thinking that time may ease the pain. It rarely does, and the firm may explode before enough partners become convinced that, if remedies are not available from within, outside help is needed.

Whether the partners can reestablish good working relationships will depend in great part on whether they can talk openly and honestly. The open dialogue must begin with the partners setting aside their egos and admitting that there are problems. A retreat using an experienced outside facilitator works well. The outside facilitator has no ax to grind or territory to protect and can offer a valuable perspective on how other firms deal with similar problems.

Candid discussion of the firm's possible fate if the issues are not satisfactorily resolved can begin to build understanding among the partners about their personal and professional goals and their attitudes toward the practice. An earnest effort at developing such understanding paves the way for building consensus to resolve the issues. It also serves as a foundation for the firm's strategic planning. Clearly defined goals can help rebuild trust among partners, enabling them to work together for the common good. Trust among partners is the firm's soul. Without a high level of trust in the firm, it is practically impossible for the partners to put the firm first—they are too busy protecting themselves.

INCOMPATIBLE PRACTICE AREAS

Another major challenge that firms face is getting practice areas to coexist peacefully. Practice areas that are extremely diverse can create mistrust and discord among the partners in the various practices. There are several reasons that practice area incompatibility is likely to surface.

- With ever increasing pressure to maximize resources and to keep a tight rein on expenses, competition for resources within a firm increases. This is particularly true when one practice area requires a bigger or more sophisticated support structure than others. For example, a commercial collection practice requires a well-run, well-staffed "assembly line" to ensure efficiency and collection of accounts. Put that practice with a criminal defense practice in which the lawyer requires little support (since much of the work is done at the courthouse and on the phone), and a likely result is the criminal defense lawyer complaining about high overhead.

- Problems are also likely to arise when a different marketing approach is needed for different practice areas. For example, a firm may decide to begin doing plaintiffs' personal injury work. Other practices in the firm might include a general business practice and a real estate practice. The partners hope that by investing resources in this new practice area, they will one day "hit the big one." Then the partners doing the plaintiffs' work want to advertise. Partners in the business practice correctly believe that advertising will hurt their image with business people in the community. Tension among partners increases and relationships suffer.

- At times two of the firm's practice areas may conflict from a business standpoint. In this context, the conflict is not a legal ethics one. The conflict results from the firm's clients having different business interests. For example, if a firm has a labor and employment practice and represents both plaintiffs and defendants (labor and management), some clients may be offended. The clients' position is that the firm may be involved in pursuing a case contradictory to their business interests. Some firms have tackled this type of situation successfully, and some clients don't have a problem with it, but the trend seems to be in the opposite direction. If clients begin to complain, then partners must make a decision about which practice to cut. This is often impossible, so relationships suffer to the boiling point, and one partner or group leaves.

- Often the level of profitability is substantially different between practice areas. Some practices are rate-sensitive or require substantial resources but produce relatively low returns on investment, especially when compared to other practices in the firm. This situation invariably leads to divisive discussions about the practice's value to the firm and about individual partner compensation.

- The level of associate support required in various practice areas can differ considerably. Any number of practices don't require sophisticated legal talent, as, for example, in slip-and-fall defense. However, if the same firm has a sophisticated transactional practice, the associates working in this practice do much more complex legal work and can command higher salaries. If a firm has different pay scales for associates in different areas, problems develop among associates and the partners who run those practices.

TECHNIQUES FOR DEALING WITH INCOMPATIBLE PRACTICE AREAS

Firms that have succeeded with "side-by-side" practices in typically incompatible areas have done so through discussing the practice in-depth *before* venturing into it. For example, a medium-sized firm in the Northeast (about fifty lawyers) decided when it was fairly small (about ten lawyers) that it would pursue a plaintiffs' practice. The partners retreated to discuss the upsides and downsides and how marketing and compensation would be handled, and many years later the firm continues to have a solid plaintiffs' practice as well as other business specialties.

Any firm thinking of adding a new practice area should pay close attention to the potential problems with practice compatibility. To the extent that these issues can be resolved, the following points are important:

- If the firm is contemplating adding a new practice area, open communication and due diligence are the best ways to avoid serious problems. Adding a practice is not unlike merging or adding lateral lawyers. It is important for the firm's management to be in a position to discuss financial implications as well as how clients feel about the practice. Partners should be informed of the downside as well as the upside of acquiring the practice. The positives may include diversifying the client base, feeding work to existing lawyers, and satisfying the needs of some existing clients. However, it is a mistake to oversell. Partners should be told just how speculative the new practice is. What will it cost for the new lawyers and their overhead as well as for marketing? What is the firm's exposure? If partners are given the worse case scenario, they are less likely to complain.

- The partners must determine how significant differences among practice areas' profitability will be reflected in compensation. The financial success of practices will vary. As long as the difference is not significant, compensation adjustments can usually be accommodated in the existing compensation system. An exception is a plaintiffs' practice. How to treat the differences here is one of philosophy. Many firms take the position that since the firm takes the risk of pursuing this work, partners should share the rewards (i.e., big fees). Typically in this type of system, the partners who bring in the work and prosecute it to a successful end may earn a generous bonus. In some firms, however, fees earned in plaintiffs' cases are handled under a different compensation scheme. How well this works depends in large part on the firm's culture, but this approach has the danger of creating a firm within a firm.

- The partners should have a solid understanding of the other practice areas and the daily challenges that confront the partners in each practice. A forum for communicating about clients and the kinds of work handled for clients can lead to a much greater appreciation of a practice's value and the partners involved in that practice.

- It is practically impossible to maintain harmonious relationships among associates if some feel like second-class citizens because they have a different compensation arrangement. The most successful approach may be to start brand-new lawyers on the unsophisticated work. In this way they can be trained and then moved into more complex work as they progress. This allows the associates to work under the same compensation scheme without hardship on the practice area's profitability. An alternative is to hire contract lawyers (not on partnership track) to do the more routine legal work. This approach can enhance profits in a marginally profitable practice as well as solve the problem of compensation among associates on partnership track.

- Some firms are able to build plaintiffs' practices by marketing through extensive networking rather than advertising. Some may advertise in legal publications to get referrals from other lawyers. Most firms that do plaintiffs' work as well as business and defense litigation generally avoid the type of advertising used by firms that do only plaintiffs' work. This is a reasonable compromise that can work.

Even with these techniques, it can be very difficult to find compromise on some practice compatibility issues. Sometimes there simply is no compromise. The practices simply do not fit. When all is said and done, often the best (and only) solution is a friendly divorce.

PROBLEM PARTNERS

It is difficult to categorize problem partners into neat little groups. The very nature of the law firm—an amorphous organization at best—makes a problem partner in one firm a way of life in another. Certainly some behavioral characteristics are not as likely to be tolerated today as they were many years ago, particularly if those characteristics could lead to malpractice problems. In any law firm, nothing can disrupt life more quickly than a partner who is unproductive, who does not produce competent work, who has a substance abuse problem, or who constantly antagonizes or creates divisiveness. Associates, legal assistants, and staff can present some of the same problems, but partners do not find it as difficult to confront such problems with these groups.

Productivity Problems

One of the most common problems is the partner who is unproductive. There are any number of reasons for unproductive partners.

- Their practice area is in a slump because of the economy or a change in the law.
- Their client base has diminished or its level of sophistication has not kept pace with the growth in their peers' client bases.

- They have been unable or unwilling to respond to changes in practice. For example, partners who have been in support roles to other partners may be unable to shift gears to originating their own work.
- They are unwilling to work as hard as other partners because of a lifestyle choice.
- They should never have become partners. Other partners do not have confidence in their work, but they became partners because the firm was unable to face up to the task of asking them to leave.
- They have become disenchanted with the practice of law. Some really don't like the responsibilities that come with partnership but feel that they have no choice but to become partners.
- They are experiencing personal problems (e.g., divorce, illness, substance abuse) that inhibit productivity.
- They are lazy and ride on their past contributions to the partnership until someone makes a fuss. They have essentially retired on the job.
- The firm has insufficient work for the number of lawyers, especially at the partner level.

Quality Control Risks

Perhaps one of the most troublesome dilemmas is the partner whose work does not meet the quality standards of other partners or, even worse, of clients. Partners who miss deadlines, don't return client phone calls, or don't do work of a high enough caliber create serious problems. In years past, problems created by these partners could usually be handled through reactive damage control. That is no longer the case. Clients now will find new lawyers if they do not receive the quality service they want and deserve. If the problems go beyond bad service, clients increasingly sue. If quality control problems are left unchecked, firms often find themselves unable to buy professional liability insurance.

The best way to eliminate quality control problems is to take a proactive approach, which means having good review systems and processes in place. In this regard, a peer review system may be the most effective prevention technique.

Disruptive Personalities

A major strength for any law firm is the strong personalities of partners. They bring to the firm many of the ingredients that make a firm successful: the ability to instill confidence in clients, to face opposing counsel successfully in trial or at the negotiation table, to lead their firms to success. The same personalities that can be such a boon to the successful firm, however, can also be a weakness. The strong egos of partners can easily cross the line, making such partners difficult to deal with on a daily basis. Some may become more of a liability than an asset. Consider, for example, partners who do the following:

- Seem opposed to anything the partnership as a whole wants to do. They are totally out of step with the firm. Often the discontent of these partners doesn't stop in the partnership meetings. They continue to complain and to torpedo a decision until a new cause comes along.
- Are abusive to staff, legal assistants, associate lawyers, and other partners. They seem unwilling or unable to extend even the most basic courtesies to those around them. The firm experiences high turnover in staff, legal assistants, and associates who work most closely with such partners.
- Refuse to follow the rules. No matter how innocuous the policy or procedure, they don't follow it. They insist on flexing their muscles only to prove that they cannot be controlled.
- Constantly threaten to withdraw from the firm if things are not done *their* way. They use their talent and their client base as a way to hold the firm hostage to get their own way or to prevent decisions from actually being made.

Substance Abuse

Substance abuse, which has increased substantially in the past few years, is a major problem in the profession. The symptoms exhibited by substance abusers include the following:

- Underproductivity
- Client relations problems or sloppy work, often creating malpractice situations (e.g., late court filings, failure to appear for hearings, missing client appointments)
- Erratic or abusive behavior that makes them increasingly difficult to deal with on a daily basis
- Frequent long weekends and abbreviated workdays because they arrive late and leave early or are out for extended periods without explanation
- Ongoing money problems, even though the partner earns a good deal and doesn't seem to spend much

These symptoms can create serious problems in law firms—in partner relationships, lost time, and lost productivity. If they are severe enough and go unchecked for an extended time, they can cause unintended departures of partners the firm cannot afford to lose and, in extreme situations, can cause the demise of the firm.

Sexual Harassment

No business can afford to ignore the issue of sexual harassment because, in addition to being illegal, sexual harassment negatively affects morale, productivity, profitability, employee retention, and recruiting. Certain aspects of the law firm environment may make firms particularly vulnerable to incidents and complaints of sexual harassment. These include long hours, frequent travel, partner autonomy, the close relationship between lawyers and their secretaries and legal assistants, the entry of large numbers of women at junior levels, and the unwillingness of those women to put up with treatment their predecessors endured. In addition, power in law firms tends to be held by men, and sexual harassment is, in large part, an issue of power—who holds it and how they use it to affect job status as well as job satisfaction. Although most firms have many women (most support staff are still female), most are in junior positions and have little power. While sexual harassment works both ways, in law firms most sexual harassment is initiated by men, simply because they are the ones typically in power.

Even in firms with well-defined sexual harassment policies, lawyers and staff are often confused about what constitutes sexual harassment and what action they should take if they feel that they are targets. Lawyers should be aware that even if some behavior may not constitute sexual harassment in the legal context, the behavior is nonetheless inappropriate. Without trying to distinguish between the two, here are examples of the types of situations that can lead to severe problems, if not legal action.

- A lawyer enters into an affair with a willing legal secretary, legal assistant, or lawyer in the firm.
- A male lawyer comments to a woman associate on the "nice legs" of opposing counsel.
- A lawyer jokes about leaving his or her hotel key for an associate.
- A lawyer asks about a coworker's relationships and sex life.
- A male senior partner comments that women are not effective litigators, although several litigators in the firm are women.
- A male partner, in discussing a matter with a client, refers to the associate on the file as "that pretty little girl over there."
- A male lawyer makes a sexist joke to see if a woman associate can take it and "be one of the boys."

TECHNIQUES FOR DEALING WITH PROBLEM PARTNERS

The single biggest challenge faced by law firm managers and leaders is addressing individual partner issues. It is harder in some firms than in others. Some firms have developed a culture in which partners are extremely frank and open with each other, making it easier to address difficult issues. In many firms, however, the opposite is true. Partners, including the managers and leaders, will go through extreme pain, inconvenience, and economic hardship before confronting individual partner problems.

Their procrastination exacerbates the problem even further. The best approach is to deal with the problem head-on.

Productivity Problems

If the problem is a recent or temporary one, discussing the reasons behind it may be sufficient. If there is no readily apparent reason for the decline in productivity, it makes sense to dig deeper, since the lower productivity may be a symptom of a bigger problem. Sometimes a reduction in compensation is enough to get the attention of partners who are unproductive because of their work ethic. Personal goal setting can also be helpful. If the situation is severe enough, it may be necessary to remove such partners from the normal partnership compensation system, placing them in a special counsel situation under a different compensation arrangement.

A partner who is underproductive because of a decline in the practice area or the loss of a significant client can usually be handled through a reduction in compensation, assuming that the partner is working to rebuild his or her practice. Partners have more tolerance for those who have lost their practices if they seem to be making an earnest effort to rebuild the practice or to "retool."

Retooling has not met with significant success, although some lawyers say that they have "retooled" many times during their careers. These lawyers tend to be entrepreneurial types who can anticipate hot practice areas and learn to become specialists in that field. Good examples of partners changing specialties this way are the real estate lawyers who became workout and bankruptcy specialists. Retooling is most appropriate when (1) there is limited, as opposed to widespread, excess capacity; (2) a particular practice area needs help and a lawyer in the firm has relevant experience; and (3) an existing practice area has a need and can afford to absorb a retooler. To be successful, however, the firm must select someone who has the basic skills and who has a great deal of interest.

Quality Control Risks

Termination may be the only solution when partners don't meet quality standards, especially if the partner lacks professional competence. If the problem relates more to the "mechanics" of practice (e.g., meeting deadlines, returning calls), there may be an underlying cause that can be corrected. One thing is certain: If a partner continuously places the firm at malpractice risk, the firm has no choice but to terminate the partner. The firm should be protected at all costs.

Disruptive Personalities

Disruptive partners are a more difficult call to make. There was a time when these partners were tolerated. Now many firms realize that the maintenance and emotional costs of keeping most of these partners are too great. Therefore, even those with strong client bases are being asked or encouraged to leave. Although some firms try to reason with these partners and suggest counseling, that approach rarely works. A reduction in compensation is sometimes effective, but for the most part termination is the only answer.

Substance Abuse

Partners who are substance abusers present a real challenge to firms. These people have an illness, and managers and leaders want to work with them to help them get well. However, if intervention is to work, substance abusers must be willing to admit that they are sick and truly want help. Many firms, working with friends and family members, do intervene, but they make it clear to the partner that unless he or she is willing to seek help, the firm will not tolerate the situation any longer.

For law firms that don't have the internal resources (including leaders who can deal with the situation), outside help is available. Consultants can help firms deal with difficult people problems. For chemical dependency problems, many state bar associations have designated individuals who serve as consultants to the firm and to the individual involved. Of course, medical professionals are also available.

Sexual Harassment

Men and women are often reluctant to file formal harassment complaints, or even to discuss their sense of discomfort with someone in the firm. This is a matter in which firm management must be sensitive and proactive. The firm is best served when the managing partner takes the initiative to suggest changes in behavior *before* a problem leads to a formal complaint.

The first and most critical step in understanding and preventing sexual harassment is developing a policy that defines sexual harassment and explains how the firm will respond to complaints. Firms don't have a choice about whether or not to prohibit the conduct, but they do have several choices about how to monitor and enforce the law. A policy that merely states that "sexual harassment is prohibited in our law firm" is inadequate. Some firms argue that a policy is unnecessary, that it is better to deal with complaints on an ad hoc basis. This is a defense mechanism to avoid addressing the issue.

Although each firm's policy and procedures may differ, the following elements should be included:

- A statement of the firm's philosophy regarding sexual harassment, which should go beyond saying, "we don't like it" or "it's illegal." The firm's goal should be to create a positive work environment for all lawyers and staff, not just to ensure that the firm is covered legally.

- A definition of sexual harassment, with specific examples of prohibited conduct. Many people think of sexual harassment in the limited sense of quid pro quo—sex for a job or promotion. However, the "hostile environment" type of sexual harassment includes a wide range of behaviors, and these should be described and discussed in the written policy.

- A statement regarding who is covered by the policy, both as harassers and harassed, which should cover all legal and support staff. It should also cover certain nonemployees, such as clients, suppliers, and the like, although liability for their actions is unclear.

- Procedures for reporting an incident, including to whom the report should be made. The firm should designate at least two people as sexual harassment officers. Larger firms should designate a committee with members from both the professional and support staffs. Sexual harassment officers should be trained in how to investigate complaints.

- Procedures to be followed in response to a complaint, including how complaints will be investigated, what type of questions will be asked, and how the firm will guarantee confidentiality and protect against retaliation.

- A description of disciplinary consequences, which might include a reprimand, referral to counseling, withholding of promotion, reassignment, suspension, termination, or an effect on compensation. The consequences should be designed to stop the harassment. The actions must deal with the problem, not just the symptoms. For example, simply transferring the harassed person will not adequately address the real problem and could be viewed as retaliation. However, it is usually important to separate the harasser and the harassed.

- A commitment to act against known harassers without waiting for complaints. Many firms have one or two lawyers whom everyone knows engage in prohibited behavior. The fact that no complaint is reported does not make the behavior acceptable. The firm has a moral and legal responsibility to take action. There is also the practical matter of client relations. If a partner is behaving inappropriately toward women in the office, he may be behaving the same way toward women in client organizations.

- Educational and training programs. Educating employees is as essential as having a written policy. The written policy is not likely to be effective if people at every level in the firm don't understand it. In many instances, offending lawyers are unaware that they are behaving inappropriately, and once they become aware that their behavior makes others uncomfortable, they are willing to change the behavior.

Firms should be careful that the goal of eliminating sexual harassment doesn't lead to other forms of sexual discrimination. For example, if, after a workshop on the subject, men become paranoid and overcompensate by not asking women to lunch or including them in other activities, they create a sexual discrimination problem. It is a difficult line to draw. Yet the more a firm educates people, the more everyone will understand the meaning and consequences of sexual harassment in the workplace.

REORGANIZING (OR RIGHTSIZING)

Law firms of all sizes have been experiencing a decline in financial performance in recent years. There are a number of reasons for this, including the following:

- Expense increases have outpaced revenue increases.
- Realization rates (i.e., ability to collect standard rates for work done) have decreased, with clients scrutinizing fees more closely.
- The firm's client base cannot support the number of lawyers in the firm.
- Competition has increased.
- Debt levels have risen (owing to partners who borrowed to pay themselves or entered into very expensive leases).
- Some partners were not held accountable for fulfilling their financial responsibilities to the firm (i.e., poor case intake, poor billing and collection efforts, poor client and project management).

Firms with strong leadership and effective management have been able to react to the changing marketplace by implementing controls to ensure stability. The firms that continue to have problems are typically those that simply cannot make the difficult choices necessary to avert continued economic decline.

Downsizing, or rightsizing, is used primarily for two reasons: (1) to save the firm from dissolution and (2) to improve the bottom line dramatically. This type of decision must be analyzed in conjunction with financial projections of what will happen in the event certain steps are taken or not taken. Outside assistance is often needed.

In a firm that is struggling economically, it is difficult to know the appropriate time to take action. It depends on the firm's culture, the extent to which partners are willing to sacrifice to keep all lawyers on board, and the extent of economic hardship the firm is experiencing. Some firms have been criticized for downsizing to maintain profits at prerecession levels. On the other hand, there are firms that, even recognizing the need to undergo a significant downsizing simply to survive, will dissolve rather than face the excruciating decisions of who will go and who will stay.

It is one thing to cut a problem partner the firm has been tolerating for years. It is quite another thing to cut a partner who, in good economic times, was perceived as making an adequate contribution. It is a heart-wrenching decision to make and even more difficult to implement. Many firms simply cannot do it and, as a result, they dissolve. Most partners, however, come to the decision that they have an obligation to try to continue the firm, regardless of how unpleasant the accompanying decisions are.

TECHNIQUES FOR REORGANIZING

Firms that must face a downsizing decision usually have one or more problem lawyers who should have been cut before the firm reached a crisis point. This is the place to start, but it is only a first step—and for firms with serious financial problems, it is rarely enough.

To head off a potentially disastrous situation, it is important to develop a formal plan of reorganization. Granted, reorganization is more of an art than a science, but the process should result in a specific plan approved by the partners. See Chapter 2 for a discussion of reorganization planning.

DIVERSITY

Law firms are not as homogeneous as they were many years ago, but many have not yet learned to integrate women and minorities into the firm with any degree of success. Few firms can boast of women and minorities in positions of leadership and significant client management and development. It is not so much that firms consciously or even overtly discriminate against women and minorities. In fact, many work hard to recruit them. It is more that the attitudes of individual lawyers have not adapted sufficiently to implement a successful program of integration and advancement for women and minorities.

Although many women and minorities cannot identify specific incidents of overt discrimination, they often feel uncomfortable. For many senior male partners, the very idea of women as professional colleagues is relatively new and a little strange. They have not yet learned to be sensitive to the types of comments, jokes, and innuendos that can make women lawyers uncomfortable. The problem is generally the same with minorities. Minorities may come from different backgrounds and cultures than do many of their Caucasian counterparts, so they may not feel like they "fit." Since this is a new experience for the senior male Caucasians, they don't know how to help with the integration process.

Business development does not come naturally to most lawyers, and women and minorities may face additional barriers.

- They may have fewer contacts in the business world. Although some male clients tell their law firms that they don't want women working on their files, time is changing this attitude. Many corporate clients that have implemented diversity policies are putting pressure on their firms to assign more women and minorities to their work.
- Because many potential clients are Caucasian males, it may be more challenging for women and minorities to develop the close personal relationships that are crucial to business development.
- In many firms partners are more likely to transition clients to younger versions of themselves.

Whatever the reasons—and there are many—behind diversity problems, firms can face an increased risk of litigation related to employment discrimination as well as sexual harassment.

TECHNIQUES FOR CREATING A DIVERSIFIED FIRM

Because it is difficult to identify the problems that contribute to a firm's inability to become diversified, there are no easy solutions. Many firms are reluctant to address the issues, often because they are not sure how to do so.

Consciousness Raising

The first step is for firm leadership to raise the issue of diversity and to engage in discussions that direct attention to the need to create a work environment in which women and minorities can be comfortable. A retreat is a good setting for these discussions. Often simply having a nonthreatening discussion helps partners focus on the need to be more sensitive to the feelings and needs of others. An outside facilitator can help the participants stay on track, ensuring that discussions deal with the issues, not with the individuals.

Policies

Every firm (no matter how small) should have written policies concerning matters involving employment discrimination. These policies must be backed up by firm leaders who are willing to confront violations. The firm's annual goals should include action plans for improving integration of women and minorities into the firm.

Role Models and Mentors

The progress of women and minorities can be negatively affected by a lack of positive role models. At most firms, there are few women and minorities to serve as mentors. By giving some thought to the purpose of the mentoring role, however, firm management can make assignments based on common interests, personalities, and characteristics. Management should monitor these assignments to ensure that the relationships are working and to make changes immediately if necessary. In addition, the managing partner should devote time to getting to know the women and minority lawyers and to discuss work assignments to help ensure that they are receiving appropriate work. This approach is more difficult in smaller firms, simply because there are fewer people. Help is usually available through bar and professional associations.

Work Allocation

Women and minorities do not always receive the same quality or quantity of assignments as their peers. With women, it may be because some of the partners feel that they are doing women a favor by not asking them to travel or to work long hours. The partners think that they are being considerate; the women think that they are being paternalistic or chauvinistic.

With minorities, the reasons are far more subtle. Especially with the firm's first minority hire, some partners are not certain how to help integrate the person. They may be overcautious in holding back on assigning travel or labor-intensive projects so that they will not be perceived as dumping unattractive assignments on the minority lawyer. The issue of work allocation becomes even more difficult in a firm where work assignment processes are fairly informal—which happens to be the case in most small and medium-sized firms. In such firms, partners assign work to those with whom they have developed personal relationships—usually younger versions of themselves.

Even small firms can formalize the work assignment process sufficiently to ensure that women and minorities are given the same types of work as other lawyers. Typically, the smaller the firm is, the easier it is not to discriminate in work assignments because there are only so many people.

Training task lists can help eliminate gender and minority biases in work assignments as well as assist in the training process. The lists describe the tasks that a lawyer in a given practice specialty should master within specified time frames (e.g., after one year in practice, after two years in practice, etc.).

Business Development Skills

Firms can help women and minorities overcome some of the business development barriers by taking several steps.

- Encouraging partners to give women and minorities as much client contact and responsibility as possible. Developing strong relationships with current clients is the best way to learn about the client relationship and to become integrated with the firm's clients.

- Taking an active role in "selling" women and minority lawyers to reluctant clients. With corporate clients, partners can push the fact that they are taking affirmative steps to create a diversified firm.
- Encouraging partners to include women and minority lawyers in business development efforts, including prospect calls.
- Training women and minority lawyers in marketing skills and providing assistance in targeting the types of relationships likely to be the most effective.

TRANSITIONING CLIENTS TO THE NEXT GENERATION

Not long ago client transition was not a major issue in law firms. Major clients were institutionalized so that when a senior partner retired, the firm could assume that the client would continue to have other lawyers in the firm handle a good deal of the client's work. Now, as senior partners retire, it is much more difficult to ensure that a client will remain with the firm. There are a number of reasons for this.

- Small firms especially (unless they are highly specialized boutiques) don't have the legal depth some clients believe necessary to service their work once the senior is gone.
- The senior may be the only one in the firm with the expertise or business savvy that the client needs.
- The senior (for any of numerous reasons) may have made no attempt to introduce anyone else to the client.

The problem is exacerbated by the tendency of many lawyers to hold client relationships tight to the vest. These lawyers may be insecure about their relationships with certain clients, about the firm's future viability, or about whether their compensation will be negatively affected by sharing clients.

TECHNIQUES FOR TRANSITIONING CLIENTS

Since the lawyer-client relationship is a personal one—regardless of whether the client is an individual or a company—introducing another lawyer into the relationship is a sensitive issue. Sometimes the client has dealt with other lawyers in the firm in other specialty areas, but if the client has had no experience with a lawyer in the specialty area of the retiring senior, the firm can easily lose some or all of the work.

Planning for the senior partner's eventual departure is a long-term issue and should include at least the following components:

- In the case of significant clients, the senior partner's annual game plan should include specific action items to begin to introduce at least one more lawyer into the client relationship. Transition works best when the partner, over a fairly long period of time, introduces another lawyer into the relationship, so that when the partner retires, the client is comfortable that there will be no change in service or competence.
- The retiring partner and the firm's managing partner (or other firm leader) should discuss the firm's desire to provide ongoing services to the client and to work with the client to select the *appropriate* lawyer to be transitioned into the relationship.
- Ongoing communication with the client during this process is essential to ensure that the client is becoming comfortable with the lawyer designated.
- The senior partner's compensation should reflect his or her willingness to be proactively involved in this process. In other words, there should be rewards for successfully transitioning clients, even if it means reduced billable hours for the senior.

TRANSITIONING LEADERSHIP TO THE NEXT GENERATION

Law firm leadership is addressed in detail in Chapter 7, but because of the subject's importance to the continued success of any law firm, it is included here with the emphasis on transitioning leadership. Leadership is a very difficult quality to describe because it is composed of numerous intangible qualities—and lawyers especially have difficulty dealing with anything they can't readily define. For that reason, lawyers are more likely to understand leadership when it is not present in their firms.

Firms too often neglect to address the issue of future leadership until the firm's leader has announced his or her retirement. Unless a "natural" successor has risen from the ranks, the firm can be left with a leadership void—a significant problem in many firms today—that can ultimately mean the death of the firm. A leadership void is most likely to happen when the leader surrounds himself or herself with lawyers dependent on the leader for clients, work, and leadership. In firms where strong partners are not nurtured and encouraged, those with leadership potential may leave. The same is true if the leader in power has a personality so difficult that partners who have the flexibility (not to mention the talent and client base) to leave will do so.

A problem can also develop if all potential leaders are the same age. The leader's retirement can create a turf battle among the contenders for the leadership position, regardless of whether one might be better suited than the others. Put another way, egos and pride get in the way of an orderly and intelligent transition.

TECHNIQUES FOR TRANSITIONING LEADERSHIP

It can be successfully argued that true leaders will ensure their succession. They do so by identifying one or more partners with leadership qualities and encouraging them to assert their leadership skills. Since a real leader must gain position in the firm through his or her behavior, day in and day out, it takes time for a young leader to instill in other partners the requisite level of trust required to become the recognized leader in the firm.

If one partner does not stand out as the obvious choice to assume the same role as the retiring leader, the firm may need to implement a different type of governance structure to spread the leadership role among several partners. This is best done, however, while the retiring leader is able to help the firm implement a different structure. For example, the retiring leader might serve as an advisor to a newly formed management group.

The firm should, ideally, develop a five-year plan for the leader's retirement. The leader should be the one to recognize when it is time to begin the plan. Otherwise, the other partners must be willing to initiate discussions with the senior leader regarding his or her plans and helping the firm in the transition.

STRATEGIC PLANNING: THE FOUNDATION FOR MEETING PARTNERSHIP CHALLENGES

Strategic planning is the process of formulating a vision—a direction toward which the firm will push its practice to take advantage of opportunities in the marketplace. Planning has been an integral part of the business world for many years. The concept, however, is foreign to most law firms. It is likely that the legal profession will continue to change rapidly. The most successful firms will be those that can anticipate the changes as well as adapt to them. That is really what strategic planning is all about—changes that can be expected and ways to take advantage of opportunities.

Strategic planning is different things to different firms at different stages of their growth and development. Consider, for example, the following:

- A start-up firm must concentrate on making the firm operational, establishing the ownership structure, capitalization, management, and partner compensation. Marketing is also a significant part of a law firm's strategic plan, regardless of any other issues that must be addressed.
- A firm in distress must direct its planning efforts toward short-term survival—developing a financial plan, downsizing, establishing strong leadership.
- Although the planning focus for mature firms should be directed toward the marketplace rather than internal issues, many firms cannot do this because of the many internal

challenges they face (such as those described throughout this chapter). If the firm has major, unresolved internal issues that have not been addressed, it is almost impossible to develop—much less implement—a strategic plan. Strong leadership, partner accountability, high-quality legal services, a fair partner compensation system, a solid practice management structure, and an environment of team play are examples of building blocks that must be present to succeed in strategic planning and marketing.

- For mature, well-managed firms, planning should take a more external focus, concentrating on specialization, practice area niches, expanded geographic locations, targeted marketing, and financial goals.

Small and medium-sized firms have limited financial and human resources and are often undercapitalized, which makes it essential for all partners to agree on their desired destination. Yet regardless of size, probably one of the most evident characteristics of successful firms is that the firms' lawyers are always working to accomplish a specific goal, like developing a new office or targeting a new client, as opposed to simply showing up for work every day. It creates excitement and energy. In that light, here are some keys to successful planning.

- Don't overcentralize the process. All partners must be involved, if for no other reason than to have them buy into firm direction. Partners who have an investment in setting goals are much more likely to be involved in implementation. The most effective strategic planning efforts are those that originate within the practice area (whether there is a practice group or one partner in that practice). Ultimately, these individual practice area plans tie into an overall firm plan.
- Coordinate the process. Although plans should revolve around the various practice areas, centralized coordination is essential. In many firms this is best accomplished by the firm's leaders, who should periodically review the plans to find ways to better integrate, implement, or enhance the plans. In addition, even in small firms all lawyers should be made aware of the plans so that they can find opportunities for joint implementation.
- Keep the plan as simple as possible. A three- to five-page list of goals and action plans for meeting those goals by practice area is far more practical than a tome that looks like *War and Peace*. The best plans are very focused on what each practice area is trying to accomplish—they don't regurgitate the firm's history, cite endless financial projections, or analyze management theories of this century. Too many firms try to emulate corporate strategic plans, not realizing that such publicly available examples are produced more for their public relations value than any true planning value.

- Avoid lofty, philosophical goals. Every firm wants "to produce the highest quality of legal work available" or "to be the best law firm in the region," but these things are assumed. They need not be included in the firm's plan. After all, no firm sets out "to produce mediocre work."

- Avoid goals that cannot be measured. If the firm does not know or cannot tell when it has achieved a goal, what is the purpose of having it? Goals that are identifiable, realistic, and backed up with specific ways of meeting the goals are most useful to the firm.

- Make goals client-driven. Since the firm's ultimate business is servicing clients and clients generally dictate the firm's success, it makes sense that the planning effort should originate around them. Businesses throughout the country routinely solicit feedback from their clients and customers as to how they can serve them more effectively. Too many law firms develop strategic plans in a vacuum, ignoring the most important source of market information, namely their own clients. Every law firm should periodically survey its top twenty-five to thirty clients to explore their future needs or plans.

- Remember the need to improve the delivery of legal services. Clients are the best source for information on how the firm can do this. Firms can double the value of their client interviewing efforts if they solicit client views on quality of service at the same time they ask for views on clients' future legal needs. For top clients, personal interviews are effective, particularly if conducted by someone outside of the firm.

- Get input from associates. Associates may have the most at stake in the planning process and may be the most affected by the firm's strategic plan. In addition, they may have some surprising, and in some cases highly accurate, comments about the way the firm manages its practice.

- Get professional guidance if it is the firm's first effort at planning.

- Make sure that the plan contains these five elements: (1) a description of the action to be undertaken and the person or group responsible for carrying out that action; (2) any personnel support from the firm or funding necessary to complete the action; (3) the date by which the responsible person or group will complete the action; (4) the ways in which the firm will follow up the action; and (5) the date on which the action will be reassessed and a determination made as to whether the action should be continued, refined, or abandoned.

- View planning as an ongoing process. Strategic plans should be revised by practice area at least once a year and preferably every six months. (This is part of the reason that good plans are short.) Revisions can be done through discussions and decisions made at firm retreats, in practice group meetings, or in partnership meetings. After such meetings, give one person responsibility for writing a brief summary of the changes.

Strategic planning for law firms does not have to be a complicated process. Often, the simpler the process is, the more effective the results. One of the best ways to begin a planning process is at a partner retreat. If the firm leaders don't have a clear idea of where the firm is headed, it is a virtual certainty that other partners don't either. It is true that successful planning requires full participation from all partners, but the impetus must come from the top.

As the legal marketplace continues to change, law firm leaders will continue to be challenged by the changes. Yet change also brings opportunity, and firm leaders who are successful in molding partner energies into common goals will turn challenges into success.

CHAPTER 2
Financial Challenges for Partnerships

Howard L. Mudrick

Among the many challenges that law firm partners have faced in the past two decades, perhaps none has been so baffling as the need to pay intense attention to the economics of running a law practice. Many firms, particularly small firms, are just beginning to learn basic financial management: income and expense budgets, profit and loss statements, balance sheets, and cash flow. At the same time, firms are faced with mounting pressure to improve the bottom line.

Many partners tend to think of financial management as completely unconnected to their practices. As a result, their firms are put in the position of having to react continually to less than desirable financial performance. The partners may realize that they face financial challenges but may not realize that, most of the time, the problems are not financial issues. They are management issues. Every management decision the firm makes, or does not make, affects financial performance. To make the best decisions, many lawyers will have to change their attitudes about the business side of the practice.

The primary purpose of this chapter is to help lawyers gain a better understanding of how they must change the way they think, the way they manage their practices, and the way they manage themselves to ensure their economic viability in the immediate future and beyond.

A LITTLE ABOUT THE BASICS

For purposes of this chapter, it is assumed that every law firm has a basic financial accounting system that generates certain reports on a monthly and annual basis. Presumably the firm has a monthly revenue and expense statement and balance sheet and other basic financial data. The reports that provide this data are listed in Appendix 1 of this book.

In addition, a consistent definition of terms common to the profession is key to any discussion of economics. Refer to Appendix 2 for a glossary of terms used in this chapter.

Lastly, there are a number of different ownership structures available to law firms, including partnership, professional corporation, limited liability partnership, and limited liability corporation. For ease of reading and to form bases for comparison, the discussion in this chapter is confined to the partnership format. Readers should convert their firm's results to a partnership form by ensuring that "net profit" (net income) includes wages, payroll taxes, and benefits (as well as any other perks) paid to the firm's owners.

THE FINANCIAL HEALTH OF A LAW FIRM

A firm's financial health is dependent, as much as anything, on how the firm manages its people and its business and, in particular, how the lawyers manage their practices. The most well-managed firms with common goals and strong cultures of accountability for practice management tend to be the most financially healthy. Since management and people issues are discussed throughout this book, discussion here is limited (as much as possible) to "pure" financial issues. Practice management issues are included throughout the chapter, because, for all practical purposes, they cannot be separated from financial issues.

What then are the characteristics of a financially healthy firm? There is no simple answer. A firm's financial health is measured through numerous financial indicators over a period of time. The most important of these indicators are discussed in following sections. Granted, some of these are more important than others. On the whole, however, a firm that scores well on the most significant key indicators of financial health can expect stable levels of profitability, as long as the firm continues to manage itself and its practices effectively.

HOW TO USE KEY FINANCIAL INDICATORS

Numerous key financial indicators, when viewed as a whole, are a good barometer of a firm's financial health. Review of the key financial indicators is only a starting point. There are no absolutely right answers here. These indicators merely help tell a story; they highlight symptoms and provide clues of where further investigation may be warranted. Once one or more of the indicators is identified as being out of line, it is important to know where to look for the underlying issue.

Use of Statistics

Testing a firm's financial health necessarily means looking at statistics. There are many available, thanks to the miracles and low cost of technology. Technology, however, may have done as much to hurt as to help financial analysis. In too many firms partners are overwhelmed with financial data they don't understand and reports they don't know how to interpret. In the sea of available information, it is easy to lose perspective. Typically in a firm where information is simply dumped on partners' desks in the same form in which the computer spits it out, partners will mire themselves in the detail, ask questions that are not particularly relevant to the firm's financial health, and draw inaccurate conclusions about what the data means. A summary of the firm's finances and key indicators is provided in Appendix 3.

Again, none of the statistics produced in a financial analysis of a law firm should be viewed in a vacuum. Many of the key indicators are interrelated. While there may be some appropriate strategies to employ to address a particular concern, the action taken may adversely affect other areas.

What follows is a description of how the key indicators can be derived and the purposes for which the statistics may be used. One of the values of these indicators is to give the firm a benchmark to compare its results to similar firms. Of course, the danger here is in determining what is "similar." A second benefit is to measure the firm's performance or change in performance over time. This allows the firm to ascertain reasons for the change.

Use of Surveys

There are numerous surveys published annually by bar associations, legal administrator associations, and consulting firms that provide comparative data on most of the key indicators discussed here. While these surveys can be helpful in measuring performance against the marketplace, firms should be careful when comparing their results with similar firms because those firms are not necessarily successful. This is a matter for particular caution when there is no way to know which firms participated in the surveys. Conversely, if the firm knows the survey participants, it is in a much better position to judge how well it is doing.

In addition, since every law firm is different, the application or appropriateness of survey data may vary from firm to firm. Allowances must be made for variances in practice areas, sophistication of the client base, and the firm's maturity, culture, and location. As a firm gains experience using these indicators, it will begin to see clear trends developing, providing information that will be helpful in making decisions, both long-term and short-term.

THE KEY INDICATORS

Following are the most important key indicators that small and medium-sized firms should use to assess their financial health.

Revenue per Lawyer

Most firms track their total fees from year to year to determine whether revenue is growing. However, simply looking at total revenue does not take into consideration the number of lawyers producing the revenue. If the revenue has increased this year over the last and the number of lawyers has increased, what does it mean? It is far more meaningful to examine revenue per lawyer. This statistic gives the firm a more reasonable basis on which to make comparisons. In addition, it is a much better indicator of whether there is any real growth relative to changes in the lawyer population. (Note that revenue for these purposes includes only fees collected and ignores reimbursements of client costs advanced and miscellaneous revenue.)

Increases in Revenue per Lawyer

Revenue per lawyer may increase for a number of reasons:

- More work
- Higher paying work
- Greater realization for the work being done
- A change in the mix of timekeepers providing the service
- Fewer lawyers doing the same amount of work
- A reduction in accounts receivable (i.e., more fees were collected during the period than were billed).

Flat or Declining Revenue per Lawyer

If revenue per lawyer is flat or declining, it is important to look at each of the aforementioned factors to help determine how to improve revenue per lawyer.

A firm may show consistent increases in revenue each year, but on a per lawyer basis, revenue may be flat or declining. This indicates that as the firm increases the number of lawyers, there is not sufficient growth in the revenue base to support these additions. In other words, the firm has grown beyond its ability to produce sufficient business to keep lawyers busy at previous levels. This is a danger signal and one that must be evaluated. Declining hours and lower realization would support this possible conclusion.

However, a firm should not be overly alarmed by a decline in revenue per lawyer without considering and evaluating other factors. For example, a healthy firm might experience declining revenue per lawyer if it is growing quickly by hiring first-year lawyers. While revenue per lawyer in this instance may be flat or decreasing, the firm may be producing greater net income owing to increased leverage, a lower cost to produce revenue, or both.

Revenue per Partner

This statistic, which has not received the attention that it should, is one of the best measures of dilution. In this context, dilution means the impact of additional partners on the total base of revenue being produced. A declining trend may indicate that the firm has added partners beyond the partners' collective ability to produce additional business. This may not pose a serious problem in the short run. In the long run, however, the expectation should be that, at a minimum, revenue per partner will stabilize. Otherwise, the more valuable partners will question the wisdom of adding new partners.

As a firm considers the acquisition of lateral partners, it must project the impact of these additions. Just as adding partners by promoting from within can cause a dilution in revenue per partner, so can adding partners from the outside. This is a statistic that needs to be evaluated over the long term rather than the short term.

Overhead Ratio

Although overhead ratio is *not* a key indicator, partners in law firms have a proclivity to use this measure, so it is listed here. This calculation is likely the most overused, misused, and poorly understood of all financial measures. As defined in most firms, it is really not "overhead" but rather a ratio of total expenses to revenue. As such, it is an extremely poor measure of how well a firm is controlling its expenses. It should never be used to compare how the firm is doing relative to "similar firms." Its value as an internal trend is to ascertain how well the firm manages its costs relative to the generation of fees. The bottom line is that this statistic provides limited management information. Instead, the firm should examine its trends, both internally and externally, on revenue per lawyer and expenses and overhead per lawyer.

Expenses per Lawyer

There are no economies of scale in a law firm. The larger a firm becomes, the greater the cost is. Highly leveraged firms invariably have greater expenses per lawyer because, by definition, a highly leveraged firm has a greater number of fee earners per partner. Since this statistic includes compensation for associates and paralegals, it is not a reliable indicator for comparisons to similar firms. This statistic is better utilized for monitoring internal trends. If the number goes up, look for the reasons. For example, has the firm hired new people? Has the firm added a new office? Have general operating expenses gone up? Has the firm failed to control expenses properly? Absent growth in the number of lawyers or new offices, if the increase in expenses per lawyer exceeds inflation, the firm should undertake a detailed line item analysis of expenses.

Overhead per Lawyer

For comparisons with similar firms, overhead per lawyer forms a much better basis than expenses per lawyer because it excludes compensation for associates and paralegals. This indicator focuses more on the cost of operations on a per lawyer basis. However, a word of caution: Just because the firm's overhead per lawyer falls within an acceptable range for comparable firms does not mean there is no room for improvement. The firm may still have line item costs that are out of line, and further examination may be in order to identify areas for potential cost savings or containment.

The major costs of operating a law firm include people (wages and benefits), space, malpractice insurance, and interest. They have the greatest impact on net income. Some quick statistics to look at include the following:

- Ratio of lawyers to secretaries.
- Total support staff to lawyers. In most small firms the ratio of support staff (which includes secretaries) to lawyers should not exceed 1:0. (One glaring exception is the personal injury firm, where staff ratios usually exceed 1:0.) To the extent support staff can be cut, there is a great likelihood that the savings per partner will be significant.
- Occupancy cost as a percentage of fees.
- Professional liability premium per lawyer.
- Debt to fixed assets. If the ratio of debt to fixed assets is greater than one, interest expense is too high.

Another word of caution: There is a point at which cutting expenses too much can have an adverse effect on client service, profitability, and firm morale. There is much truth in the old adage that you have to spend money to make money. For example, if lawyers and paralegals spend too much time doing their own clerical work (sending faxes, making copies, etc.), their productivity may suffer. If secretarial ratio is very low, stress and illness can be major factors in the ability to service clients.

Net Income per Partner

Many believe that this is the only statistic that matters. It is important because it illustrates how well the firm is doing in creating income to be shared by the partners. It is also often important to the individual partners because it allows them to measure their performance against partners in similar firms. In effect, it is how the partners keep score.

Too often, however, firms equate success with an increase in net income per partner. In fact, this lone statistic is given far too much weight. This is because, by definition, this number focuses only on what the average partner earns rather than what a partner making similar contributions can earn in a similar firm. Put another way, even if net income per partner is on the rise, if it is not competitive in the marketplace, the most productive and valuable partners could be subject to cherry picking.

A decline in net income per partner should not necessarily be viewed as a negative. For example, when a firm adds a new partner from within, the expectation should be that in the short term the average net income per partner will decline, since the new, lower-paid partner drives down the average.

Profitability Index

The profitability index is a measure of how effectively the firm is able to convert fees collected into income for the partners. It measures the firm's ability to utilize others to generate fees that ultimately produce net income. To calculate the index, divide net income per partner by revenue per lawyer. The greater the result is, the better the firm is utilizing its timekeepers to generate revenue (and profits). Here is a sample calculation:

Net income per partner	$170,000
Revenue per lawyer	$200,000
Profit Index	.85

The most successful firms have a profit index greater than 1.00. (It is important to carry the result to two decimal places to arrive at a result that can be compared.) This measure is very important because, from both an internal and external vantage point, the firm is able to assess how well it is doing at managing its resources to produce a profit return to the partners. As a management tool, this statistic is getting nowhere near the attention it deserves.

Numerous variables can affect the profit index, including billable hours, rates, realization, and leverage. This statistic, more than most others, should be monitored over a period of years. Increasingly, successful firms are incorporating a profit index goal as part of their strategic plans.

Billable Hours

Billable hours continue to be the basis on which most firms bill. In well-managed firms, billable hours are monitored monthly to project cash flow and to find out who is working and who is not. A decrease in billable hours invariably translates to reduced collections some time in the near future.

Billable hours analyses should be carefully correlated to other indicators discussed here. If, for example, revenue per lawyer falls below comparable firms, a natural place to start is with billable hours. However, the analysis should not stop at a comparison of average billable hours by timekeeper class. A more useful internal tool might include a comparison of actual billable hours to budget and an examination of the number of timekeepers recording hours below budget. An examination that shows departures from expectation (below budget) is likely to be a far more useful internal management tool than a simple comparison of averages to similar firms. The comparison of averages is best used to form a global benchmark for comparison. However, the analysis should not stop there. Individual performance must be monitored regularly.

Exhibit A. Calculation of Realization

	Value of unbilled time at the beginning of the year	$250,000
Plus	Fee accounts receivable at the beginning of the year	$300,000
Plus	Value of billable time worked during the year (valued at agreed rates)	$1,000,000
Minus	Value of unbilled time at the end of the year	$275,000
Minus	Value of accounts receivable at the end of the year	$250,000
EQUALS	Potential fees to be collected	$1,025,000
	Fees collected	$900,000
	Realization Fees Collected/Potential Fees To Be Collected	87.8%

Realization

Realization is one of the most important yet least used indicators in law firms today. Realization is defined as the relationship between the value of billable hours recorded and the actual fees collected for those hours. Exhibit A provides a detailed example. Sophisticated software packages can calculate realization by client, matter, or even lawyer.

This statistic is useful because, from a management standpoint, it allows the firm to measure how well it is collecting for the resources allocated to a project and how effectively the firm is collecting established prices. What this statistic does not do, although many partners believe it does, is tell the firm whether the work is profitable. Realization ignores the cost to produce the work, a needed ingredient for testing profitability.

Aged Unbilled Fees

It is important to review unbilled time monthly. The focus should be especially critical on matters for which unbilled time exceeds ninety days. This should raise a red flag because, as ninety days pass, it means that the client was not billed at least on a quarterly basis. Absent an agreement in writing with the client to the contrary, the firm's expectation of collectibility will become suspect when billing is not done at least quarterly.

Aged Accounts Receivable

It is very important that aged accounts receivable be monitored monthly, since this is the final stage before an invoice gets paid. Managing accounts receivable is a critical element in short-term cash flow planning. When amounts are outstanding over longer periods of time, it is less likely that the full amount will be collected.

Inventory Turnover

Calculating inventory turnover is crucial to cash flow planning. It indicates on average the amount of time it takes the firm to convert a billable hour into cash. The results of this calculation often surprise firms because they believe the average turnover time to be considerably less than reality. A firm that has a turnover of 150 days is on average collecting in June the time worked in January.

To improve collectibility of billable time, the firm must work hard at reducing inventory turnover to the lowest level possible. A firm that has low inventory turnover frequently has high realization and a high profit index. It is billing more frequently, and clients pay more quickly. Fewer questions about bills are likely, resulting in fewer write-offs. This in turn means greater revenues and therefore greater net profits.

Client Dependency

It is important to examine the amount of fees received from each of the firm's top clients each year. Depending on firm size, look at fees received from the top ten to twenty clients each year. This tells the firm the extent to which it relies on a small number of clients to provide a volume of fees. The extent to which any one client represents more than 10 percent of a firm's fees in a particular year is important in evaluating the vulnerability that a client this size creates for the firm. Likewise, it is important for a firm to monitor which clients are in the top ten to twenty from year to year as well as the trends in fees received from those clients. A decline in fees may indicate an unhappy client or the completion of a one-time matter. Monitoring fees from its top clients puts the firm in a better position to budget and to plan.

Debt and Capital Ratios

Balancing debt and the need for capital from partners is an issue that law firms confront continually. Debt should not exceed the book value of fixed assets. To the extent that bank borrowing exceeds the book value of fixed assets at any point in time, the firm is relying on the bank to pay partners. By way of illustration, consider the following example:

Furniture and fixtures	$100,000
Leasehold improvements	$100,000
Computers	$70,000
Library	$20,000
Depreciation	($150,000)
Book value of fixed assets	$140,000
Bank loan	$125,000
Line of credit	$50,000
Total debt	$175,000

Paid in capital	$50,000
Undistributed earnings	$100,000
Total Capital	$150,000

Since total debt exceeds the book value of fixed assets, this firm is relying too heavily on bank debt. It has borrowed $35,000 to pay partners.

This firm's debt to equity ratio is greater than one. This means that the partners have relied to a greater extent on external financing ($175,000 from bank borrowing) than on funds provided from partners (paid capital plus undistributed earnings) to operate their business. With a ratio greater than one, banks are less likely to grant favorable terms for borrowing.

THE NEED TO IMPROVE PROFITABILITY

Law firms are caught in a catch-22. The unparalleled changes that the legal profession has experienced in the past decade have taken big bites out of a firm's ability to increase its bottom line. While partners are at least as demanding as they have ever been in their income expectations, in most firms the result will be that the average partner will not earn as much as he or she earned in the past.

Most firms, even the most financially successful, have been on an expense-cutting, cost-control journey in recent years. Many were in a position to cut fat and realized significant improvements in their bottom line for a year or two. Once expenses are under control, however, firms can improve profitability only by increasing revenue. (Simply raising rates no longer works.) Improving revenue is quite a challenge in an environment where the following factors exist:

- Clients are in control. Clients are now making the rules, and they are changing them with great regularity. This means that there is little room in most firms for raising prices.
- There are too many lawyers for the available work.
- Clients are demanding improved quality service (they always deserved it—they didn't always get it), and they are looking carefully at whether they get value for the service.
- Disgruntled clients are becoming more adversarial. If it is determined that the client has been overbilled, the firm may be lucky to get off by simply "forgiving" the receivable.
- Clients are interested in value billing. This is a difficult concept for lawyers who have been accustomed to being paid for the hours they work, not necessarily the value they give the client.
- Clients are interested in alternative pricing, but to many clients that means fixed fees, contingent fees, task-based billing, or discounts. (For more on this topic, see *Billing Innovations: New Win Win Ways to End Hourly Billing; Win-Win Billing Strategies* and *Beyond the Billable Hour*, all edited by Richard C. Reed and published by the ABA Law Practice Management Section, in 1996, 1992, and 1989 respectively.)

- Clients do not want to pay for associate training. Although small firms have never been able to achieve the leverage ratios of larger firms, it is even more difficult today. Clients believe a major advantage of working with smaller firms is that they can deal directly with partners.

Many of today's client realities are the antithesis of the behavior that hourly billing brings. For firms with profits insufficient to satisfy partners, the only solution may be working harder and smarter, assuming there is sufficient work.

PRACTICE MANAGEMENT'S EFFECT ON PROFITABILITY

Once expenses are under control, the best place to look for ways to improve profitability within a firm's existing structure is in practice management. Individual partners' management of their practices has the single biggest impact on profitability.

Good practice management is not a plentiful commodity in the legal marketplace. Lawyers want free rein in deciding which clients to represent, what to charge for the work, who will do the work, whether to specialize, and how to bill and collect for their work. All these things have a tremendous impact on profitability. Some partners see the economic losses that result from poor practice management habits as an occupational hazard that partners must accept. This is a dangerous attitude, and one that can spell disaster for any law firm.

Simply put, practice management is the management of lawyer and paralegal resources in the delivery of services to clients. It provides a vehicle for the orderly operation of the following functions, which play major roles in the firm's future success:

- **Work acceptance guidelines:** Partners have an understanding of the type of work they will do and what they will charge for it. They make sure that clients have the ability to pay before they begin work. Many ask for retainers for certain clients or certain types of work. A partner doing corporate work does not accept a litigation matter without consulting the litigation partner. Work acceptances guidelines are set out in Appendix 4.
- **Billing and collection guidelines:** Partners use written fee agreements and discuss the fee and the firm's billing practices with the client up front. The partner has an open discussion with the client about the client's goals for the work and how much that is likely to cost. The client understands that the firm expects to be paid within the agreed-on time frame. Billing and collection guidelines are set out in Appendix 5.
- **Billing and collection process:** In well-managed firms the accountant never hears, "I'm too busy to do bills." The firm has a billing process, and partners adhere. In addition, receivables are "worked" aggressively. Once a receivable is

thirty days old, someone in the firm is responsible for calling the client, and there is regular follow-up through the time of collection.

- **Timekeeping:** Time is recorded daily to ensure that all time is captured and that the time recorded is the time spent. This is an important element of profitability, since most firms will continue to do significant time-based billing in the foreseeable future. Timekeeping is equally important, however, in task-based or fixed-fee billing because it forms the basis for computing the cost of the firm's services.

- **Associate and paralegal production:** It is the partners' responsibility to ensure that associates and paralegals have sufficient work, that the work is supervised properly (to satisfy clients and to minimize time write-offs), and that associates and paralegals are trained. In well-run firms partners do not do associate or legal assistant work—a common cause of time write-offs. In addition, associates do not do legal assistant work. In very well-run firms (the exception), all timekeepers know their budgets and what is expected of them.

- **Specialization:** Each lawyer becomes known for a specific specialty area, and all work in that area goes to the designated lawyer or lawyers. While this approach is key to marketing success, it also helps keep fees in line because the specialists do not have to reinvent the wheel.

- **Client service:** Lawyers in well-managed firms pay significant attention to their clients, and they communicate with clients frequently. They do not rely on clients to inquire about the status of their legal work. They spend time understanding each client's needs and building relationships. Strong client relationships help avoid questioned bills and lagging receivables.

- **Increase in pricing:** Firms can raise prices—without raising hourly rates—through increased specialization, innovation, and technology as well as by finding ways to add value to the services they offer clients.

- **Reduction in the service delivery cost:** This can be done through a continuous process of improving the management of client work, by increasing leverage (i.e., delegating) to the extent possible (especially to paralegals), and by avoiding duplication of effort. More effective use of technology is key.

- **Increase in volume:** Increasing volume simply means working harder, and many partners are now doing this.

WAYS TO ADDRESS KEY FINANCIAL CHALLENGES

Other chapters in this book discuss the tremendous changes taking place in the legal industry, the need for law firms to adapt to these changes, and the need for effective management and strong leadership. Chapter 1 relates the many challenges facing law firm partnerships today. Most of these are directly related to the financial challenges that confront law firms.

Some of the more troublesome issues for law firms today were unheard of in years past. Regardless of the cause behind them—inadequate financial acumen, poor decision making, lawyers' refusal to change their attitudes, or simply fate—these challenges test the skills of the firm's leaders and the relationships among the partners. Some of the problems are not easy to solve. Depending on the problem's severity, solutions range from "tightening the belt" to downsizing and restructuring.

Revenue (Fee) Budgeting

Ask ten managing partners of small or medium-sized firms whether they have a budget, and nine will say that they do—and that they perform within 2 or 3 percent of budget annually. Ask the same group whether their budget includes fee projections, and only two will answer yes.

In preparing their annual budget, most small firms pay the greatest attention to the expense side and little, if any, to revenue projection. This is largely because forecasting expenses is very easy compared to predicting revenue with any degree of certainty. Yet revenue forecasting is critical to projecting cash flow and the amounts available for distribution to partners.

There are different approaches to projecting revenue, and none is perfect or without some guesswork. This holds true for the following approach as well. Nonetheless, this technique provides a starting point for firms that bill on an hourly basis. A detailed illustration of the calculations is provided in Exhibit B on page 62.

1. Prepare a schedule showing billable hours for each timekeeper for the past three years. Based on an examination of the trends for each timekeeper, project a billable hour amount for the coming year.
2. Multiply each timekeeper's projected hours by his or her current hourly rate. The result is the accrual revenue projection, assuming a 100 percent collection rate of time at stated hourly rates.
3. Total the amounts for each timekeeper projected in step 2 and apply the firm's historic realization factor to this total. *Note that realization is the critical element for computing a realistic revenue projection.* Applying a realization factor introduces reality to a calculation that is based simply on multiplication. That is, realization rates tell firms what is ultimately collected versus what is recorded as chargeable time.
4. The total fees determined now equal an accrual amount that ignores the length of time it takes to bill and collect for time. To account for this timing difference, use inventory turnover to convert accrual fees to cash basis fees.

Exhibit B.   Sample Revenue Budget

1. **ACCRUAL REVENUE PROJECTION**

	Hours	Rate	Revenue
Partner 1	1,500	$200	$300,000
Partner 2	1,700	$180	$306,000
Partner 3	1,600	$180	$288,000
Partner 4	1,600	$175	$280,000
Partner 5	1,500	$160	$240,000
Associate 1	1,600	$120	$192,000
Associate 2	1,600	$100	$160,000
Associate 3	1,450	$120	$174,000
Paralegal 1	1,200	$50	$60,000

   Total Accrual Revenue Projection $2,000,000

2. **INVENTORY TURNOVER (TIMING)**
   12/31/xx inventory (work in process and accounts receivable)—
   Work in process = $350,000
   Accounts receivable = $450,000
   Average monthly value of billable time worked = $2 million/12

   Turnover = *(work in progress + accounts receivable)* × 30 days
   Average monthly value of billable time worked
   Turnover = 120 days

3. **COMPONENTS OF CASH BASIS REVENUE**
   a. Accrual revenue forecast = $2,000,000 (before realization)
   b. Billing Realization = 90%
      Collection Realization = 95%
   c. Turnover (timing) = 120 days

4. **COMPUTATION OF CASH BASIS REVENUE FORECAST**
   a. Inventory reduced by realization rate:
      $350,000 × 90% × 95% = $229,250
      $450,000 × 95% = $427,500
                              $726,750
   b. Accrual revenue forecast reduced by realization rate and by timing
      $2,000,000 × 90% × 95% × (365 − 120)/365 = $1,147,800

5. **TOTAL CASH REVENUE FORECAST**
   $726,750 + $1,147,800 = **$1,874,550** (amount of fees this firm can expect to collect during the year).

5. To forecast cash basis revenue, start with the projected inventory at the end of the current year. Apply the firm's billing and collection realization factors to each inventory (work in process and accounts receivable) to determine the collectibility of the existing inventory.

6. To the amount calculated in step 5, add what is likely to be collected from the accrual fees (in steps 1 through 3) for the

coming year. This amount can be computed by multiplying accrual fees by 365 (days) minus inventory turnover divided by 365 (days). This total reflects how much of the time worked in the coming year will be collected during the year.

Having a fee budget as well as an expense budget gives the partners a projected net income for the firm, which in turn translates into their compensation. By monitoring the firm's performance against the budget, the partners gain very specific information about what they must do to meet income goals. This approach can be a strong motivator for partners. Monitor variances monthly to determine whether the firm is on target, looking at each element, including hours, realization, and turnover.

Cash Flow

Cash flow management is a significant challenge in most law firms. In small firms it is a particular concern, since, for the most part, partners want to take out as much cash as possible as quickly as possible.

There are any number of areas where firms can spring leaks in the cash flow process. The potential holes include the following:

- Lack of understanding by the client regarding when payment is expected. While much has been written about increased client demands, little is discussed about the expectations law firms should have of clients in terms of timely payment of invoices.
- Failure of the firm to bill in a timely manner.
- Failure to follow up on receivables and slow-paying clients.
- Desire of partners to pay out available cash quickly. By drawing out all available cash, partners leave their firms vulnerable to the ebbs and flows of future cash flow and the demand for operating expenses and advancing client disbursements from that available cash.
- Inadequate budgeting and planning. Few firms plan their cash flow needs beyond meeting the next payroll. As part of the budgeting process, every firm should prepare a cash flow projection that shows anticipated cash needs on a monthly basis. Then each month the firm can monitor what is in the pipeline in terms of projected cash based on outstanding receivables and the potential for collecting them.
- Inadequate reserves for one-time payments or for unusual expenses, such as an extra payroll during the odd month or annual payment of property tax.

Practice Management Factors. As discussed earlier, practice management has a greater impact on law firm profitability—and cash flow—than any other aspect of the firm's business. The work acceptance process sets the stage for the business relationship between the firm and the client. Beyond that, managing the work properly, getting the work done on time, keeping the client informed of the status of the work, billing in a timely manner, and managing collections of accounts receivable all play a major role in the regularity of cash flow.

Partner Draws.   Draws must be realistic and based on available cash—not on what the partners need to meet personal commitments. Most well-managed firms keep draws to partners as low as possible (e.g., 60 to 80 percent of anticipated compensation) and distribute excess cash available on a quarterly basis. Low monthly distributions to partners means that the monthly cash requirements are lower, resulting in less demand for short-term borrowing to meet monthly operating needs. In fact, some firms defer distribution to partners when there is not enough cash. Other firms distribute only what is remaining after paying expenses and retaining an adequate amount of cash to meet a portion of the next month's operating expenses.

Funding: Debt and Capital

Debt (bank borrowing) and capital are the means by which a law firm provides dollars to fund the business. Capital includes contributions from partners and undistributed earnings.

Adequate Levels of Capitalization.   It is difficult to make general statements about adequate levels of capitalization without knowing the specific needs of the law firm. However, undercapitalization is a frequent problem. Too often firms depend on bank borrowing to fund their operations. This creates a hazardous situation when revenue or cash flow decreases at the same time that profits decline.

Debt.   Debt must be examined on a regular basis. A fiscally responsible firm will limit its borrowing to fund the purchase of fixed assets (furniture and equipment).

Firms that continually rely on line-of-credit borrowing to fund their operations are playing with fire. These firms are, in essence, borrowing to pay partners in anticipation of future collections. This creates a mortgage on the firm's future, since many firms cannot rely on timely collections of their receivables. To eliminate the mortgage, firms that borrow on their line of credit should reduce the borrowing to zero for at least sixty consecutive days each year. This check-and-balance approach helps assure that the firm does not rely totally on the bank to pay partners and instead relies on firm profits to generate income for partners.

The Need for Working Capital.   To help reduce the need for bank borrowing, firms need working capital to operate. Working capital is different from the capital needed to fund the acquisition of furniture, fixtures, and equipment. It provides cash for the day-to-day operations of the business, including cash advances on behalf of clients, funding growth, smoothing out collection cycles, and providing a short-term cushion. As owners of a business, all partners should contribute capital.

Amount of Capital a Firm Needs.   Just how much capital does a firm need? There is no formula that provides the answer. It depends on the following:

1. Anticipated purchases of fixed assets less bank borrowing contemplated to fund those purchases, plus
2. Any increase in net advances on behalf of clients (advances made plus reimbursements received), plus
3. The inventory turnover multiplied by the cost of projected growth.

By way of illustration, consider the following example:

Annual cost of adding a lawyer: $50,000
Firm's inventory turnover: 150 days
Capital Need: $50,000 × 150 divided by 365, or about $20,500

Several variables affect the cash flow impact that a firm can expect with a new hire.

- The new lawyer's level of experience
- The collectibility of the lawyer's work while he or she is being trained
- The quantity of work available to the lawyer once the lawyer is trained, factored in with the hourly rate and realization, as well as the amount of time it takes to bill and collect
- Any additional rates of return the firm can expect in subsequent years as the new lawyer gains experience
- The new lawyer's income expectations and the rate at which the firm will continue to give the lawyer compensation increases. This means that the partners must either contribute additional capital to fund this growth, use a portion of profits to fund this growth, or both.

The method of a capital contribution can involve having partners write checks (which may mean that they must borrow the money personally) or withholding a portion of the partner's income over a period of time. The method chosen depends on the capital needs of the firm. For example, if the firm is planning to hire additional lawyers, the need for additional capital is immediate. Therefore, the best option is for partners to write checks. As an alternative, deferring distributions of profit can be a less painful way to accumulate the necessary working capital.

A firm's method of covering its capital needs depends in large part on its culture and on its fiscal philosophy. Some firms do not borrow at all. Others borrow to pay for fixed assets. The extent to which a firm borrows for growth and to even out cash flow depends on how conservative or liberal the partners are in their attitudes about borrowing. Each firm must find the balance that is right for it. It is more prudent to err on the side of conservatism by having partners contribute to the capital needs of the firm rather than to rely on the bank to be the significant provider of funds.

Too Many Partners for the Book of Business

Historically, the traditional attitude toward partnership admission was that once a lawyer had spent a certain number of years in the firm, he or she deserved to be a partner. No thought was given to how a new partner would affect the take-home income of other partners. Most firms were able to attract more business and raise rates to keep partner income stable and to add associate leverage. Then suddenly, firms of all sizes found themselves with some partners who, while reasonably competent technically, could do little to develop business or expand existing business. Often the lawyers did not continue to develop professionally and could not handle work at the level of sophistication necessary to attract business. As a result, firms were left with partners doing associate work at associate rates, but earning or expecting to earn incomes at partner levels.

In the short term, this type of partner has an adverse effect on profits. In the long term, the partner fills a "slot" in that practice (in small firms, he or she may be the only partner in that practice area), making it impossible to grow the practice effectively.

Many firms today find themselves with too many partners for their book of business, with no reasonable prospect of turning the situation around. They may or may not have other financial troubles. If, however, a firm's net income is so low that the most valuable partner or partners are threatening departure, the firm may have no choice but to outplace (terminate) underproductive partners. If the situation has lingered long enough, additional downsizing may be necessary.

The more fortunate firms have the opportunity to "close" the gate and to take a different direction by following any of three paths. First, they can implement an agreement among the partners concerning the criteria new partners must meet to be admitted. Such criteria may include the following:

- Excellent lawyering skills, quality work and quality service to clients, and the respect and confidence of lawyers in the firm
- Good client relations skills and good business judgment
- Ability to provide work for other timekeepers in addition to one's self, by bringing in new clients, by retaining and expanding work from existing clients, or by managing a large volume of client work
- Ability to manage multiple projects simultaneously and to do the work in a profitable manner

- Adding value to the firm, either through a unique practice expertise or quality

A second course is to analyze the long-term economic impact (e.g., over three to five years) of adding another partner, regardless of the talents of the associate being considered for partnership. This requires answering several questions.

- Does the firm have a sufficient book of business to justify the addition?
- To what extent will partner incomes be diluted, and for how long?
- Has the associate demonstrated the potential to develop new clients or to expand business from existing clients?
- Does the associate add value to the partnership through an important practice expertise?
- Is the associate's professional development such that the partners expect that his or her development will continue to progress?
- What is the economic impact or client service impact of the associate leaving if he or she is not made a partner?

A third course available to firms in this situation is the implementation of a two-tiered partnership or another alternative to equity partnership. (For a detailed discussion of two-tiered partnerships, see Chapter 5.)

Unproductive Lawyers

Another continuing challenge for firms comes in the person of the unproductive lawyer. Small and medium-sized firms, because of the close personal relationships among lawyers, have more difficulty dealing with this problem—and often don't until they are in a crisis situation. For purposes of this discussion, unproductive lawyers are those who exhibit one or more of the following symptoms:

- Have low billable hours
- Have unprofitable practice areas
- Work at rates below their expected levels (e.g., the partner who works at associate rates)

There are innumerable reasons for underproductivity that go beyond the scope of this chapter. (Chapter 1 discusses the subject in more detail.) Regardless of why lawyers are unproductive, one thing is certain—the effect on the bottom line can be significant. In a very small firm, one unproductive lawyer can make the difference between the firm having a good year or a bad year.

The best way to deal with the problem is head-on. The firm's leader should meet with the lawyer to let the lawyer know that his or her level of production is a problem. The solutions vary, of course, depending on the circumstances and the severity of the problem.

- If the reason is simply that the lawyer is not working hard enough, the choice is obvious. The lawyer can work harder or choose to leave. The decision becomes his or hers. Sometimes the lawyer is relieved to have the opportunity to leave gracefully.
- If the lawyer is working hard but simply not recording the time, training can solve the problem. It is simply a matter of correcting a bad habit.
- If the firm does not have enough work to keep that lawyer busy, then the firm must decide whether the situation will change soon enough to warrant keeping the lawyer.
- If the lawyer is working below his or her level of expected competence, the best solution depends on whether the lawyer is a partner or an associate. If the lawyer is a partner who has been with the firm for many years, the solution may lie in a different compensation arrangement or in a different role (e.g., an of counsel position). If the lawyer is an associate who is simply not progressing as expected, the firm should be candid with the associate and terminate employment.

Client Pressure to Reduce Fees

In response to continued client pressure to keep fees down, firms have watched their realization rates and leverage decline. Law firms simply can no longer assume that they will be able to collect 100 percent of the time they record or bill or that they can enjoy associate leverage as in years past. Clients are increasingly drawing their lines in the sand.

- They are no longer willing to pay for associate training or for reinventing the wheel, so they are scrutinizing bills carefully.
- They are no longer willing to pay for large staffing on cases. They want experienced people to manage the work with as few lawyers involved as possible. This attitude has helped dilute the opportunity to leverage with associates and paralegals. Small firms have seldom been able to achieve the large associate to partner ratios that large firms have. Nevertheless, leverage has been important to small firm profitability. Significant leverage—in the traditional sense—may be a thing of the past.
- They are no longer willing to pay for time if the time spent is not accompanied by value. More clients are applying pressure to get discounted rates (especially if they offer volume work in return), fixed fees, or task-based billing.
- They are no longer willing to pay higher rates each year. As a result, the hourly rates in many firms have remained fairly stagnant for several years.

- They are no longer willing to give firms carte blanche on fees. Clients expect budgets for the work the firm will do and expect their firms to do the work within the budget.

Well-managed firms are responding to this pressure by improving practice management and by seeking innovative ways to manage and delegate work and to have strategic plans focus on more sophisticated, specialized work to enhance earning power. Part of the firm's strategic plan must include ways to leverage without large numbers of associates. This can include use of trained legal assistants, work product retrieval systems, forms files, product development (e.g., software programs for specific practice areas), and document assembly programs.

During this pricing transition, many firms will have decreasing profits. For some the only way to increase profits will be to work harder. For many others, however, partners are already working as hard as humanly possible. For those firms careful planning will be vital.

Unprofitable Practice Areas

Historically, it was not unusual for a firm to support an unprofitable practice area. Perhaps the practice was one that provided services to many of the firm's clients. For example, the firm may have kept an estate planning practice because it served as a loss leader for bringing in additional work. It is more difficult to rationalize keeping unprofitable practices today because the cost to produce legal work has risen and the client pressure to reduce fees has increased. In addition, many practice areas that have traditionally been profitable no longer are for many firms.

Just what is an unprofitable practice? Ask five people and they will give five different answers. For the most part, lack of profitability is caused by a combination of one or more of the following:

- Low billable hours because there is too little work, the lawyer or lawyers doing the work are not working hard enough, the lawyer or lawyers doing the work are not recording time accurately, or the client is only willing to pay for so much time
- Low rates, typically because the market will not bear higher rates
- High overhead for the practice, often because the lawyer or lawyers in that practice are being paid more than the rates justify
- Low realization
- Poor case intake, case management, billing, and collection practices

Defining profitability is difficult because there is no "right" or "scientific" way of determining the cost of services. Firms that have been doing it for some time now began by feeling their way around and ultimately developing a methodology that works for them. The key is for the partners to agree up front on the assumptions that will be made to arrive at an answer. Ideally, this will help minimize grousing about the results. The following is one methodology to consider. Exhibit C provides a detailed example.

1. Calculate "direct costs" allocable to each timekeeper, including salaried partners, associates, and legal assistants. Direct costs include wages, including overtime and bonuses; payroll taxes, including FICA and federal and state unemployment taxes; and benefits, including insurance, pension and profit sharing, workers' compensation, and similar items. *Note that direct costs do not include any amounts paid to equity partners.*

2. Calculate "indirect costs." Take total expenses (net of any reimbursed expenses) and subtract the total amount allocated as direct costs to the timekeepers (from step 1).

Exhibit C.   Profitability Analysis

	Weighted Index		
4 Partners	1.5 = 6.0		
3 Associates	1.0 = 3.0		
2 Legal Assistants	0.5 = 1.0		
	10.0		

Associates	Wages	Benefits and Payroll Taxes	Total Compensation
A	$40,000	$8,000	$48,000
B	$50,000	$10,000	$60,000
C	$60,000	$12,000	$72,000
Legal Assistants			
X	$20,000	$4,000	$24,000
Y	$25,000	$5,000	$30,000
			$234,000
Other Operating Costs			$566,000
Total Expenses			$800,000

Timekeepers	Direct Cost	Indirect Cost	Total Cost
P1		$120,000	$120,000
P2		$120,000	$120,000
P3		$120,000	$120,000
P4		$120,000	$120,000
Aa	$48,000	$80,000	$128,000
Ab	$60,000	$80,000	$140,000
Ac	$72,000	$80,000	$152,000
PLx	$24,000	$40,000	$64,000
PLy	$30,000	$40,000	$70,000

3. Prepare a full-time equivalent count for all timekeepers by class. "Full-time equivalents" are those who have worked twelve months out of a year. A timekeeper working six months is counted as one-half. Then multiply the number of full-time equivalents by a weighted index for each timekeeper class as follows:
   - Partners × 1.5
   - Associates × 1.0
   - Legal Assistants × .5

   The weighted index is an approach to allocate indirect costs to each timekeeper on a basis that approximates their uses or demand for firm resources. For example, a partner typically has a larger office than an associate or legal assistant.

   Perhaps the biggest controversy on allocation of indirect costs is how to allocate them fairly. Should the legal assistant be allocated overhead costs at the same level as a partner? Not according to this approach. This approach assumes that partners consume a larger share of the overhead than the associates, who themselves use a larger share than the paralegals.

4. Calculate indirect costs for each timekeeper class. Divide indirect costs (from step 2) by the total indexed amount (from step 3). Then multiply the result by the weighted index for each classification (i.e., partners at 1.5, etc.). Note that each full-time equivalent timekeeper within each class has an equal indirect cost allocation.

5. Calculate total costs for each timekeeper by adding his or her direct costs (from step 1 above) to his or her indirect costs allocation for his or her timekeeper class (from step 4).

This analysis is not precise, as mentioned earlier, and it is best used to test results over a period of time rather than for a one-year snapshot. It is not designed as a model for determining individual profitability. It is a management tool, designed to test the profitability of practice areas, individual clients, and matters. It is also designed to help a firm determine its costs for purposes of evaluating alternative pricing.

Once a total cost is determined for each timekeeper, divide that amount by the average expected billable hours for that timekeeper class. The result is the cost per hour for each timekeeper. Recognize, however, that the cost allocation for equity partners includes only their share of overhead and not an amount for draws or distributions.

An additional step is to examine the fees collected, for example, from a specific client or a practice group or area during the year. Most billing software packages make it possible to determine the number of hours that each timekeeper recorded for the fees collected. Multiply each timekeeper's hours by their costs per hours, and compare the total costs to the fees received. If the fees exceed the costs, it means that the fees more than covered allocated costs, with some left over to pay the partners. If the costs exceeded the fees collected, the fees were not sufficient to cover the costs to do the work, let alone to make any payment to partners.

Unfunded Liabilities for Buyouts

Many law firms today find themselves in a situation where their level of unfunded liabilities (e.g., amounts owed to departed and departing partners) could destroy their firms. These liabilities may have been created for the buyouts of partners' interest in the firm when a partner voluntarily withdraws, retires, or terminates owing to disability or death. Some firms have limited this liability by buying insurance to cover death and disability and by implementing qualified retirement plans that partners fund out of current earnings. Even so, many firms are left with the potential for significant benefits being paid to departing partners out of future earnings.

The buyout often consists of a payment for the partner's interest in work in process and accounts receivable or a fixed amount (e.g., one to two times the partner's average compensation over a several-year period). The firm then pays this amount to the partner out of future earnings over a period of time. This philosophic approach worked reasonably well for many years because few partners left a firm except for retirement, disability, or death, and the presumption was that firms would continue to grow. Since growth tended to be fairly certain, the buyouts did not place a heavy burden on future earnings.

Transitioning to a Pay-as-You-Go System. The challenge arises in trying to transition from large unfunded benefits (buyouts) to more moderate benefits funded on a "pay-as-you-go" basis through a combination of insurance policies and partner contributions. Older partners especially have relied on the promise that they would be paid retirement benefits by the firm. Because they have been paying for benefits, mid-level and younger partners also believe they are entitled to these benefits when their turn comes to leave the firm. There must be an agreed-on cutoff point for partners entitled to receive these benefits.

The first step in addressing the problem is for the partners to recognize that it is a problem. Partners who have been counting on these benefits want to believe that the problem does not exists.

The next step is to analyze the complexity and magnitude of the obligation and to determine whether it is possible simply to eliminate unfunded benefits or whether a plan of transition is necessary. Whatever the plan, the firm's tax advisor should be involved. Some possible solutions used by firms include the following:

- If partners did not "buy in" (i.e., pay for their partnership interest in accounts receivable and work in process) and all partners are fairly young (e.g., forty-five or younger), the partners may simply agree to rewrite the partnership agreement, providing for a cash basis buyout. In essence, departing partners would receive their paid-in capital accounts and earned but unpaid compensation.

- If the partnership agreement provides for the payment of a share interest in work in process or receivables, a different type of transition could be negotiated. New partners would be brought in on a cash basis (i.e., they would contribute a fixed amount to capital and would be returned their capital when they leave the firm). The current partners would agree to a fixed payout of work in process and accounts receivable on the books on a certain date and paid by a certain date, which amount would be fixed and not changeable. The amounts might be paid over a five- to ten-year period, using the partners' current interest in earnings. This type of transition places less cash strain on young partners and provides for a fixed amount, while at the same time it protects the firm against heavy cash drains because of departing partners. The payout in effect is a part of overall compensation.

- An alternative might be to discount work in process and receivables to present value, assuming a ten-year payout and 8 percent interest. The firm would borrow the money and pay it out immediately. Each partner would be entitled to an amount equal to his or her compensation share multiplied by the present value amount. This alternative separates the payout from compensation, but it does require that the firm incur debt. It should not be used unless the debt is less than the current value of fixed assets. The additional debt to fund this amount reduces cash basis equity. The repayment of the amount borrowed will reduce the cash available for distribution to active partners in future years.

- Another alternative would be to freeze the current work in process and receivables at their current levels, deducting appropriate amounts for uncollectibility, but defer payment until each partner leaves the firm.

Regardless of the alternative used, any amounts to be paid to departed partners should be subject to a limitation of payments provision. Such a stipulation provides that payments to departed partners will not exceed a specified percentage of the firm's net profits in any one year. Amounts in excess of the limitation are deferred proportionately over ensuing years.

Funding for Some Benefits. Firms should consider purchasing disability and life insurance policies to cover benefits for disability and death. Care must be exercised before purchasing these types of policies, and partners must be clear about the benefits being provided related to the cost of the policies. In addition, firms should consider implementing some type of qualified retirement plan. This is the approach that the best-managed firms use. In effect, partners themselves fund a substantial portion of death, disability, and retirement benefits. (For more on this subject, see Chapter 4 of *Getting Started: Basics for a Successful Law Firm*, 1996, the first book in this series.)

High Occupancy Costs

Many law firms are saddled with occupancy costs that they cannot afford. The high costs are a result of entering into office leases during an inflationary period and committing to too much space in anticipation of continued growth. It goes without saying that the amount a firm can afford to pay for space depends on its level of profitability. An effective test is to compute the firm's occupancy costs as a percentage of fees and to compare that number to similar firms in the general geographic area. A reasonable range is 8 to 10 percent. If space costs the firm more than 10 percent of fees, it is likely to be more than the firm can afford.

Since a lease is typically involved, there is no easy solution to this problem. If the firm has excess space, it can sometimes sublease the space to other lawyers or professionals or, in a popular building, the landlord is sometimes willing to take back the space. The only other alternative is to attempt renegotiation of the lease. What can be accomplished in renegotiation depends on the circumstance. For example, sometimes extending the lease for another five years or more can bring concessions. If the firm is in financial trouble and can demonstrate that it may not survive without rent relief, the landlord may be more willing to rework the lease. The landlord is not likely to renegotiate a lease when partners have not taken every step possible to improve their condition. Sometimes the only solution is to tighten the belt and to ride it through.

Reorganization or Downsizing

For many of the reasons previously discussed, a firm can find itself in the unpleasant position of having to downsize to survive. Some firms have used this solution simply to improve the bottom line, but in small firms especially, this approach can be divisive and can destroy the fabric of the firm. Most firms use this approach as a last-ditch effort to save the firm from dissolution

Firms that face dissolution are usually suffering from a number of problems. As a result, there is no way to advise a firm about when it should take action. How soon the firm acts will depend on its culture, how much partners are willing to sacrifice, and just how economically deprived the firm is. Even in the face of dissolution, some firms do not have the stomach for making very difficult decisions and will dissolve rather than go through the pain of deciding who will go and who will stay.

Almost always the firm has one or more problem or unproductive lawyers (typically partners) who should have been cut before the situation became critical. Getting rid of these lawyers is an obvious starting point, but if the situation is serious enough, this will not be enough.

A Plan of Reorganization. After the obvious cuts of problem partners, the firm must begin by developing a formal reorganization plan. There is no prepackaged plan that will carry a firm through a financial crisis. The solution depends in large part on the problems that gave rise to the crisis. There are, however, key elements to include.

- In small firms, involve all partners in the adoption of the plan. In large firms, get support from practice leaders as well as the firm's leadership group.
- Analyze three years of financial information and compare results to similar firms in the marketplace. This information will help the firm set realistic financial goals. (See the earlier discussion of key financial indicators.)
- Develop several "what-if" scenarios of revenue and expense projections. These will provide projections on net income and individual partner compensation. Ideally, the compensation goals will be realistic. However, only the partners can decide whether they will be happy with this level of compensation. If the partners are unhappy with their projected income, or if they see a significant differential compared to other firms, dissolution may be the only alternative. The partners must be involved here.
- Determine the approximate number and mix of timekeepers that will be needed to service the firm's current volume of business. With substantial clients, this evaluation must consider client relationships. This is not to say that lawyers with client relationships should be exempt. It does mean, though, that the firm must measure the impact on revenue of anticipated loss of business. What-if scenarios are helpful in this analysis.
- Develop a list of lawyers who should be cut—partners and associates. Cutting associates only is not likely to help sufficiently. In addition, cutting too many associates can produce long-term problems for client work that requires less experienced lawyers.
- Cut any existing fat from expenses. Remember that most expenses are fixed, so, unless the firm has allowed expenses to go uncontrolled, there is not often much relief available in this area, except in people (lawyers and staff) and rent. Often lease renegotiation is essential to a viable reorganization plan.
- Make all cuts at one time. Otherwise, morale suffers greatly. Many firms make the mistake of making cuts one at a time over an extended period. This approach creates an environment in which it is assumed that cuts will continue. As a

result, lawyers and staff alike are more focused on when it will happen to them rather than on doing their work.

- Prepare for morale problems. When a firm reduces staff—even to survive—morale problems will emerge. This is a time for strong leadership. The firm's leaders must help remaining lawyers and staff understand that the cuts were necessary for survival and that the focus must now be on servicing clients.

LONG-RANGE GROWTH PROJECTIONS: LOOKING TO THE FUTURE

When firms consider their long-term growth options as part of strategic planning, they rarely analyze the economic consequences of various options. Too often firms fly by the seat of their pants. Long-term financial forecasting is especially critical in a small firm because the economic impact of decisions is likely to have a greater impact on the firm's bottom line. There are fewer partners among whom to spread the risk.

As discussed in other sections, growth has a negative impact on current cash flow. That is, as a firm hires new lawyers, the firm must plan for an outlay of cash for some period of months before cash collections will be realized. Likewise, as a firm promotes lawyers to partnership, it must examine the long-term ramifications to ensure that it understands the impact on available profits. This sort of financial forecasting need not be overly complex, yet it should include a forecast beyond one year. Here is an example.

New associate annual salary	$60,000
Benefits and payroll taxes	$12,000
Total cost	$72,000
Turnover 120 days	
$72,000 \times 120/360 = $24,000	
Impact on Cash Flow during First 12 Months	

When a firm promotes a lawyer to partnership, projections must consider the following:

- The quantity of partner-level work that the firm has for the new partner
- The partner's hourly rate, realization, and time to bill and collect
- The partner's expected income for the next several years

CONCLUSION

Ensuring a firm's future economic success is not merely a function of knowing how to read the firm's financial statements. Future success depends on numerous elements, not the least of which are the following:

- Planning, especially financial forecasting to ensure that management decisions make economic sense. This includes hiring new lawyers and promoting additional lawyers to partnership.
- The partners' willingness to manage their practices for profit enhancement. This includes adapting to client demands and expectations and to different methods of pricing and work acceptance, along with effective client communication, staffing, and collection of receivables.
- The partners' willingness to contribute working capital to their business.
- A conservative approach to bank borrowing.
- A firm culture in which partners' accountability for their contributions to the firm is a given. This includes accountability for billable hours, revenue generation, profitability of work, and expansion of work.
- A willingness to change to adapt to the marketplace, particularly the demands and attitudes of clients.

Those firms that understand that financial performance is the result they obtain from their management and practice management decisions are the ones that will stay the course.

CHAPTER 3
Protecting and Nurturing the Institution

Berne Rolston

A growing law firm will eventually reach a stage where the focus must change from the goals of individuals to the preservation of the law firm as an institution. In many firms the original partnership agreement does not adequately address matters that are critical to an institutional firm. This chapter focuses on those matters. Smaller firms contemplating long-term growth may benefit from addressing the issues raised in this chapter as well.

In the context of firm growth, it is important to distinguish between the goals of the group and the goals of the individual. The emphasis in an institutional law firm must be on the protection of the entity (and therefore the combined goals of the firm's principals). This may mean that individual goals are, of necessity, sublimated to the needs, goals, and objectives of the organization.

A law firm's partners must determine whether they will practice together in effect as "roommates," with no obligations beyond the need to pay their share of the "rent" on a monthly basis, or whether they will institutionalize the firm by in effect entering into a "spousal" relationship, with all of its attendant long-term benefits and obligations.

No business organization can survive as an institution unless it has developed the following characteristics:

- A solid and adaptable financial and personal infrastructure
- Workable methods of governance, with a strong, centralized, and responsive management structure devoted to protecting and enhancing the institution without doing unnecessary harm to its individual members
- An adequate capitalization method to meet its current and future needs
- A process for selecting and disciplining its principals as well as for assisting the individual members of its constituency at their various life cycles

This chapter addresses the principal and more important conceptual issues that need attention in the partnership arrangement.

- Partner selection
- Partner termination
- Indemnity by terminated partners
- Payments to former partners
- Liability of former partners
- Professional liability
- Disability
- Retirement by seniority

While these issues should be addressed in the initial organization of the firm, lawyers in growing and well-established firms should take a second look to assure that these issues are properly covered in firm policies or in the partnership agreement.

PARTNER SELECTION

At the heart of any law firm are the partners and those who aspire to become partners. As used herein, the term "partners" refers to any lawyer who is an owner of an interest in a law firm, regardless of the form of its organization. In an age when law firms cannot afford to maintain unproductive partners, poor partner selection can have serious effects on the long-term health of the firm. Good partner selection is just as important in the continuance of an existing firm as it is in organizing a new firm. The attributes expected of a partner and his or her continuing obligations to the firm need to be considered and publicized.

Criteria for Choosing Partners

To help evaluate whether a proposed partner will make continuous meaningful contributions to the well-being of the firm, lawyers organizing a firm or considering merger should ask the following questions in nine key areas:

1. **Values, beliefs, and vision**
   - Does the individual have views similar to those of current partners with regard to the nature and interrelationship of the firm's constituencies and the firm's long-term vision?
2. **Productivity**
   - In terms of client work, will the individual be effective and efficient in the performance of billable functions?
   - In terms of supervision, will the individual be genuinely committed to the delegation of work to other partners and the firm's professional staff?
   - In terms of client relations, what is the extent and quality of the individual's communication with clients? Will the

individual project effort and concern for clients' problems, and is there any evidence of client concern? Will the clients of other lawyers voluntarily "return" to the working partner, as distinguished from the originating partner?

3. **Office participation and relations**
   - What is the extent of communication, attitude toward, and working relationships with partners, associates, legal assistants, administrators, and other nonlegal staff?
   - Will the individual willingly share with and delegate to other partners, associates, administrators, and nonlegal staff?
   - Will the individual participate in the training of others?
   - Will the individual genuinely support the management policies adopted by the firm?
   - Will the individual participate in professional and community affairs as part of a personal commitment to contribute to society?

4. **Billing and collecting responsibilities**
   - Will the individual discharge billing responsibilities properly and voluntarily?

5. **Timekeeping**
   - Have all essential timekeeping records always been current and thus accurate, mostly current, mostly late and thus inaccurate, or always late and mostly fiction?

6. **Recruiting**
   - Will the individual undertake responsibility for recruiting willingly and ably, or reluctantly?

7. **New business development and retention**
   - What will be the extent of the effort (not necessarily the result) made to develop business from existing clients and new clients?
   - Will the individual be committed to finding, minding, or binding?

8. **Ethics**
   - Is the individual in the firm's "mainstream" insofar as ethics are concerned, both as a lawyer and as an individual?

9. **Team play**
   - Will the individual be truly part of the team or tend to do his or her "own thing" with little concern for others and the firm as a whole?

While it is highly unlikely that any existing or proposed partner can lay claim to full satisfaction of all these criteria, this does not mean that these criteria are not useful as yardsticks. The objective use of these questions to measure how each existing or proposed partner meets or will meet his or her obligations to the firm forms a fair basis for the evaluation of each partner's existing or potential contribution to the firm.

Associate to Partner

Conversely, many associates may not know what is expected of them to become partners in the firm. To avoid the unnecessary disappointments that may result from misunderstandings, either by the firm or by the prospective partner, the firm's membership criteria must set forth *publicly*, and preferably in writing, the factors the partners will consider in deciding whether any given associate should be invited to join the firm. Clear, unequivocal guidelines will avoid unstated expectations on either side. They should focus on two main areas.

1. **Eligibility:** The policy of a firm should be that associates be considered eligible to become partners on the basis of their individual merits, affirmatively demonstrated over a stated period of time. As a general guideline, associates should not be considered for partnership until they have been in actual practice as lawyers for a given period, which customarily is from five to seven years (and in some instances even longer). Similar guidelines should be applied to lawyers hired laterally, except that those lawyers need only to have been with the firm for a period of time sufficient to ensure a thorough evaluation (usually a period of three to five years from the date of first employment).

2. **Specific guidelines:** Once an associate is considered eligible on the basis of time in practice, these additional guidelines should be considered in determining whether that person should be invited to become a partner.

   - The associate has demonstrated affirmatively that he or she possesses attributes that would enhance the firm if the associate became a partner. The associate has reached a sufficient level of maturity, both as a person and as lawyer, so that no doubt remains as to that person's ultimate importance to the firm.
   - The associate has reached that level of expertise where he or she is already a competent lawyer, able to handle most matters with minimal supervision.
   - The level of mutual respect between the associate and the existing partners would allow a partner to conclude that the firm will continue to function smoothly as a group when this person becomes a partner.
   - The person is highly regarded in terms of stature or reputation in the community, among other lawyers, and among the firm's clients.
   - The associate is likely to develop new business for the firm or to play a significant role in the satisfaction, retention, and expansion of existing clients.
   - The associate will be able to supervise and train other lawyers.
   - The associate will satisfy a need within the firm and contribute to its well-being.

- The partners would be proud to have this person introduced to others as their partner.

The firm should emphasize publicly that the foregoing are guidelines only. They are not criteria or standards to be applied rigidly. Consider what the word "guidelines" implies: a course that, when followed, leads to the desired result. If properly used, the publication of such guidelines should bring more objectivity to the partner selection process, help reduce any "popularity contest" aspects, and provide associates with something more than vague hopefulness.

Continuous Application of the Guidelines to All Lawyers

Clearly, a firm should apply its guidelines for the admission of new partners with care. It is equally important to continue to assess how existing partners measure up (i.e., peer review). From the firm's point of view, the basic issue is: What does this person mean to or do for the institution to enable it to continue as partners come and go?

Over the years a group of partners may have been elected who had sufficient time "in grade"; worked moderately hard; satisfied most needs assigned to them in terms of work effort; had satisfactory relations with clients, other partners in the firm, and staff; and are worthy of being hired by other partners for the task for which they have become trained. In such instances, a firm may have created a class of partners who, while technically satisfying the published guidelines, may not have the necessary spark to assure the firm's continued vitality and progress. In time such partners may become so numerous as to dissipate the effort, viewpoint, and goals of the partners who are in fact the energy source of the firm.

While many of the "partners' virtues" set forth positively in the guidelines can and may have been met, the firm as a group must find that the person in question clearly satisfies the following characteristics:

- Provides substantial business to the firm
- Spends more than average hours on client matters
- Has particular expertise in an important area of practice
- Is capable of total independent action in the area in which he or she practices
- Is a strong participant in firm affairs
- Is willing to do what is necessary

Otherwise, that person is not or never will become one of the energy sources for the firm's growth and health and, in fact, may become a deterrent.

From the largest to the smallest, law firms are beginning to understand that the marketing of their services requires multitalented persons as partners. "Nice guys" can finish first. The fact is, however, that merely being nice is not enough—it must be coupled with commitment, drive, energy, dedication, effort, and personal growth. Firms must continually focus on how each lawyer's attributes—or the lack of them—does or will affect the firm.

The business of practicing law is a continuous evolutionary process, and each firm should give serious thought to the question of its future dependency on and symbiotic relationship with those it elects as its partners.

Those in leadership positions in law firms must learn to select and continually evaluate partners carefully on a proper continuing basis and to establish and maintain an equitable compensation system. Otherwise, law firms will continually be faced with the erosive loss of good partners and the consequent deterioration and even destruction of their firms.

PARTNER TERMINATION

In addition to choosing partners carefully, the firm must be prepared to end its relationship with a partner under certain circumstances. In the operation of any business, the enterprise must have the inherent power to protect itself by discharging or disciplining a participant if the enterprise, after appropriate consideration, determines in good faith that the partner has violated the standards or criteria for partner performance.

Therefore, the partnership agreement should provide that a partner may be expelled for cause by appropriate vote of the other partners (excluding the vote of the partner whose expulsion is under consideration), if that partner engages in any of the following activities:

- Is disbarred or suspended or is the subject of any other major disciplinary action (Note: If a partner is disbarred, it is essential that the remaining partners vote to expel to avoid violating ABA Model Rule 5.5, which prohibits lawyers from being in partnership with a nonlawyer. Some firms may make disbarment grounds for automatic expulsion from the firm.)
- Engages in professional misconduct or violates the *ABA Model Rules of Professional Conduct*
- Engages in any action that injures the professional standing of the partnership, if that action continues after a request to desist
- Is declared insolvent or bankrupt or makes an assignment of assets for the benefit of creditors
- Breaches a major provision of the partnership agreement, if after written notice, the breach continues or occurs again
- Habitually lacks attention to the business of the partnership
- Fails to file any state or federal tax return
- Commits an act of willful misconduct or gross negligence resulting in a loss to the partnership

Great care must be exercised in the process of disciplining or expelling a partner, and the due process rights of the affected individual must be carefully preserved and followed. Express provisions in that regard should be set forth in the partnership agreement.

DEPARTURE DISINCENTIVES

Law firms have looked for ways to protect themselves from withdrawing partners who would compete with them by taking clients from the firm. Rule 5.6 (a) of the *ABA Model Rules of Professional Conduct* reflects the prevailing view: "A lawyer shall not participate in offering or making a partnership or employment agreement that restricts the rights of a lawyer to practice after the termination of the relationship, except an agreement concerning benefits upon retirement." The rationale behind this rule is apparently that restrictions on the right to practice limit a client's freedom to choose a lawyer. The rule has been applied to covenants not to compete in employment contracts as well as to partnership agreements.

Some firm partnership agreements have included disincentives to departing partners who choose to compete against their former firm. The theory behind such provisions is that they are liquidated damage clauses; the departure of a partner causes harm to the organization and the partners have a right to establish in advance the value of damages produced by the harm. The firm might suffer damages in any of the following ways:

- The firm has recruited personnel, and acquired space and equipment to operate, and in so doing, each partner has relied on the continued contribution of the other partners.
- The firm and the partners have committed to a certain course of action and to certain liabilities in reliance on the continued operation of the firm.
- To the extent a withdrawing or expelled partner takes firm clients, the firm and the remaining partners may be damaged.
- To the extent a withdrawing or expelled partner takes other partners, associates, or staff, the firm and remaining partners have been damaged in an amount equal to the expense of recruiting and training of replacements.
- After the withdrawal or expulsion of a partner, the continuing firm may have excess space, staff, and overhead.
- After the withdrawal or expulsion of a partner, the pro rata share of each remaining partner's liability will increase.
- Certain costs may directly result from the departure.

To make matters more problematic, in suits by departing partners, some courts have construed liquidated damages clauses to be noncompete clauses and have refused to enforce them, thereby defeating the intent of the partners. The evidence suggests that today more lawyers are willing to sue their former firms than in the past if they believe that the partnership agreement does not give them the full value of their equity in the firm. Certainly, a formula giving all classes of departing partners full value for their interest in the firm is least likely to be challenged. Even a punitive provision that is applied to all departing partners—not just the competing ones—is not likely to be challenged because it can be argued that since the provision applies to all departing partners, it is not a covenant not to compete. Provisions that treat departing competitors differently from retirees, deceased partners, or other withdrawals are most likely to be challenged. Firms that want to protect themselves from partners who continue to practice law in the same market as the existing firm need to be very careful in drafting their liquidated damages clauses providing such disincentives.

The best advice is to avoid any reference to competition, loss of business, or economic protection of the firm in the disincentive provisions. The language should focus explicitly on the business losses that will be occasioned by the departure of a partner. The terms should state that the signatories to the agreement have been fully informed of these provisions and that they are agreeing to them freely.

This view is reflected in recent cases. The traditional and majority view that disincentive clauses penalizing departing competing partners violate Rule 5.6 and that such clauses are unenforceable is reflected in cases such as *Cohen v. Lord, Day & Lord*, 75 N.Y. 2d 95, 550 N.E. 2d 410, 551 N.Y.S. 2d 157 (1989), and *Weiss v. Carpenter, Bennett & Morrissey*, 672 A.2d 1132 (N.J. 1996).

Other courts have been more willing to uphold the partners' agreement to penalize departees. In *Hackett v. Milbank, Tweed, Hadley & McCloy*, 654 N.E. 2d 95 (1995), the agreement called for a reduction of benefits if the departing lawyer earned more than $100,000 per year. The court upheld the plan on the ground that it was "competition neutral" and not in violation of Rule 5.6. California adopted an even more supportive stance in support of law firms against departing partners in *Howard v. Babcock*, 6 Cal. 4th 409, 863 P.2d 150, 25 Cal. Rptr. 2d 80 (1993). The California court held that the rule banning restrictive covenants does not prohibit a withdrawing partner from agreeing to compensate his or her former partners in the event he or she chooses to represent clients previously represented by the firm. Such a construction appears to represent a sensible balance between the competing interests of the law firm and the departed lawyer. On the one hand, it would enable a lawyer to withdraw from a partnership and continue to practice law anywhere within the jurisdiction. The lawyer would also be able to accept employment should he or she choose to do so from any clients who desire to retain that lawyer. On the other hand, the remaining partners would remain able to preserve the stability of the law firm.

Whether cases like *Hackett* and *Howard* represent a trend away from striking down disincentive clauses is not at all clear. These cases do suggest that careful drafting may permit law firms to achieve their objectives with respect to departing partners, despite the elevated risk of litigation. In light of these developments, law firms should give serious consideration to the negotiation for and entry into appropriate agreements that would be a disincentive to withdrawal and a strong stimulus to dissident parties to find solutions to their problems, thereby providing protection to the economic stability of the firm. Because the case law varies from state to state, however, firms must be sure to examine local law on this issue.

Aside from cost and damage to the firm and the monetary and capital debt issues, upon the unhappy event of the withdrawal or expulsion of a partner, other matters must be dealt with in advance. These include the following:

- The disposition of the firm's records and files, particularly vis-à-vis the clients' rights in that regard
- The compensation for allocation of the completion of work that has already been undertaken by the firm on behalf of clients who have chosen to depart with the withdrawing or expelled partner
- The appropriate possession of files, documents, and other records and matters pertaining to clients

INDEMNITY BY WITHDRAWING OR EXPELLED PARTNERS

Careful thought should be given to the need for all partners to agree in the firm's partnership agreement that, in the event of a partner's expulsion or withdrawal, the partner should indemnify all remaining partners and the firm and hold the remaining partners and the firm harmless from all liabilities resulting from the conduct of the departing partner during his or her tenure with the firm. The same applies as well as to those liabilities and resulting damages and direct or indirect costs arising from his or her withdrawal or expulsion from the firm.

EASING THE ECONOMIC IMPACT OF PAYMENT TO FORMER PARTNERS

In addition, the manner or nature of the withdrawal must affect the manner in which the firm deals with the repayment of the amount calculated to be due to a withdrawing partner. A retiring partner should be no threat to the law firm's economics (assuming there are no unfunded retirement benefits). Departure by death can be dealt with through insurance proceeds, which is highly recommended, rather than burdening the living partners of the firm with the obligation to acquire the interest of the deceased partner. A withdrawing partner intending to practice law in the same community, however, does offer (as discussed earlier) an economic threat and potential damage to the firm.

Great care must also be taken in considering the *manner* in which the agreed-on capital or other debt owed to any departed partner is repaid. Appropriate limitations on the amounts payable during any given period must be considered, such as an annual cap based on a percentage of income or profit that could be used to pay departed partners. In addition, it would be appropriate to provide for payment to a retiring partner over a shorter period and payment to a withdrawing/competing partner over a much longer period. In any event, provisions must be contained in the agreement itself as to what should be done under those circumstances.

EXISTING AND FORMER PARTNERS' LIABILITY FOR PARTNERSHIP DEBTS

Firms must consider how to deal with the issue of a departing partner's liability for his or her share of the firm's debts and how to provide that such a departing partner shall have no liability for the debts of the firm incurred *after* the date of his or her departure (although this alone will not deter the claims of third parties). Some organizational agreements provide that a departing partner remains liable for his or her pro rata share of the current and long-term obligations existing at the time of departure to the extent that such debts cannot be offset against any payments due that partner or may not be paid from firm assets as such debts become due, whether or not such a partner was a signatory to any contracts, debts, or other liabilities in existence before departure.

However, special consideration is often given to a partner whose departure has occurred because of death, disability, or retirement, perhaps to join the judiciary. These partners are often treated differently and perhaps should not be responsible for any debts or obligations of the firm, no matter when incurred (beyond those included in the calculation of the partner's cash basis capital account or net accrued assets capital account, if any). The firm may hold the departed partner free and harmless from any further share of the obligations of the firm, except for those obligations incurred by that partner that were tortious or not authorized by the firm.

PROFESSIONAL LIABILITY

Most firms consider that the only nonoperating liability a firm may suffer will arise out of an act of malpractice by a partner and that the use of insurance will deal with the problem of such costs. Rarely do agreements provide for the sharing of noncovered losses, that is, the cost of deductibles or the resulting liability for the gross negligence or willful misconduct of a partner (including acts resulting in sexual harassment, workplace discrimination, or other forms of personal tortious conduct), or claims made after a partner has left the firm arising out of events that occurred during his or her tenure with the firm. This leaves the resolution of such matters and the resulting cost to the application of common-law indemnity to deal with the impact on the other partners. Similarly, situations created by the departure of partners, either voluntarily or through expulsion, retirement, or death, must be treated differently. For example, it might be appropriate to limit a retired or deceased partner's share of such liabilities to any act arising in the four years preceding that partner's retirement or death. These issues should be considered in advance and appropriate provisions be provided in the firm's management documents.

DISABILITY

Most law firms deal with disability on the basis of an insurable risk, but few deal with the manner in which or how it is determined that the lawyer involved is disabled or how the cost is shared if insurance coverage is limited or nonexistent. To minimize the risk of having to maintain at its expense a lawyer who in fact makes no contribution because of his or her disability, an institutionalized firm will create and publish a disability policy. Depending on the circumstances and the extent of insurance carried by the firm (or the individual partners, depending on the nature of the firm policy to be adopted), such a policy should, at a minimum, contain the following:

- The definition of "disability" (e.g., "a partner is 'disabled' when he or she fails to devote normal time to partnership affairs because of any physical or mental condition").
- A *maximum* "permissible period of disability" (perhaps ninety days) during which the firm will continue the regular or normal periodic payments (draws/salary) to the disabled partner without adjustment of his or her interest in the profits and losses of the firm.
- An "extended permissible period of disability" (perhaps an additional ninety days) beyond the initial period upon condition that the affected partner neither receive nor accrue any draws, salary, income, or benefits during that second period.
- A partner's disability that (1) extends beyond the permissible periods of disability or (2) is caused by a chronic physical or mental disorder, in which case the disabled partner should be deemed to be permanently disabled and to have withdrawn from the firm. His or her partnership interest should be purchased by the partnership on the same terms applied to the purchase of such partnership interest from the estate of a deceased partner without the application of any insurance proceeds.

The policy might also provide for periodic or intermittent disability to be cumulative (perhaps ninety days within a nine-month period) subject to adjustment to the affected partner's participation in the firm's profits to reflect the level and value of such a disabled partner's productivity.

In any event, to the extent that the firm has paid a partner during any period of disability, it should receive credits or the benefits of any insurance in effect, either the firm's or the individual partner's.

In no event should the firm be obliged to make any payments to or share any profit with a disabled partner beyond the maximum permissible periods unless such payment obligations are appropriately funded.

RETIREMENT BY SENIORITY

Retirement of partners poses three major questions in law firms today.

1. Should the firm have mandatory retirement?
2. What retirement benefit, if any, should the firm provide, and more important, will the benefit be funded?
3. How does the firm retain as much of the retiring partner's "know-how" as possible?

Mandatory Retirement

Many firms have a policy of mandatory retirement. The reason that many other firms do not have a policy is that they do not address the issue until one of their partners reaches retirement age. This is the wrong time to deal with the matter. Once a firm is faced with a specific situation, the decision becomes an emotional one rather than a business one. The best time to deal with retirement is when all partners are still fairly young. No firm that intends to institutionalize its being can do so without a stated retirement policy.

The advantage of a mandatory retirement policy is that the firm, rather than the individual, is in control of the matter. While many partners who reach retirement age (usually sixty-five to seventy-two years of age) remain eminently qualified to practice, many do not. A written policy allows the firm to protect itself by easing out partners who simply no longer should or want to be in practice.

To provide for an orderly retirement process for seniors, many firms provide for a transitional period before retirement (e.g., three to five years) in which the partner phases out of firm management and transitions clients to others in the firm. During that time, the compensation of the retiring partner is reduced to reflect his or her changing role in the firm.

Many retired partners want to continue to be involved in the firm after their retirement. An of counsel relationship permits this. Each year the retired partner and the firm negotiate a plan of contribution outlining how the retired partner plans to spend his year and how he or she will be paid for that contribution. The retired partner can continue to transition relationships, market the firm, serve as a teacher or consultant to young lawyers, and essentially spread the firm's goodwill in the business and legal communities.

Retirement Benefits

Many law firms in the United States have partnership agreements that commit the firm to paying substantial retirement benefits to retiring partners. That is, retiring partners are paid out of the firm's future earnings. A huge disadvantage to this approach is that the firm must remain economically viable for the retiring partners to receive their benefits. Often the economic burden to the firm is so great that remaining partners are unwilling to continue to make the payments. In fact, war stories abound (and some litigation) about law firms that dissolved because of large unfunded benefits due to departed partners.

There are a limited number of options. The partners could agree that they will "take home" less and thereby contribute to some type of retirement plan. This type of "funded" approach is known as the "pay-as-you-go method." Essentially, all partners contribute to their own retirement benefit. Some lawyers object to this method because they feel that the firm should provide a benefit. The fallacy to this argument is that the firm as it currently exists may not be around to provide the benefit, and then the retired partner will be left with no benefit.

The other option for a firm that does not fund retirement benefits is to have the partners agree that each individual partner will be responsible for his or her own retirement planning. The biggest disadvantage to this method is that often the individuals do not provide for their retirement, so when the time comes they cannot "afford" to retire and must continue to work, even if their legal skills and judgment have deteriorated. This presents a problem for the remaining partners, who must either force the senior out of the firm or face possible malpractice problems.

In any event, the best advice to any firm, particularly to one just being formed, is to *avoid unfunded benefits* of any kind at all costs.

Retaining a Senior's Know-How

Too many firms have realized after the fact that when a senior has retired from the firm, the firm has suffered more than expected because they did not plan for the senior's retirement. Senior partners are a major firm asset, often in more than one way.

- They serve as firm leaders, often as the "glue" that binds a firm together. This leadership can be a major firm strength and when it is no longer available, can have devastating results for the firm. In this situation, a transition period allows the senior to "pass the mantle" to a partner who, with the right support, can gain the respect he or she will need to bring the firm forward.
- They control major clients by virtue of their relationships with those clients that have evolved over many years. A transition period, with a well-designed plan for each major client

of that partner, may help the firm keep clients they might otherwise lose. The plan would include the designation of the partner who will become the client manager, with a plan of action for how the designated partner will be phased in as the client manager. Part of the plan might include a way of introducing more than one lawyer to the client to enhance the relationship.

- They have stature in the business and legal community. This is a more difficult role to transition and one that usually takes years, but, through a series of introductions in the right places, a senior can help ease the way for firm lawyers that follow him or her.

CONCLUSION

Regardless of what choices a law firm may make in the face of the issues discussed in this chapter, it is essential to the institution's preservation that each issue be confronted and dealt with "up front" so that an issue's irresolution shall not sow the seeds for later discontent and the possible destruction of the fragile fabric of the firm.

CHAPTER 4

Firm Governance and Management Structures

Ezra Tom Clark, Jr.

A firm's governance and management structure is the key to meeting and taking advantage of many of the changes and challenges facing law firms. That structure exists on three levels.

1. **Governance:** This level focuses on the issues that involve the control, direction, and policies of the firm. It also involves selecting the individuals who will manage the firm. Decision making at this level is usually made by the owners.
2. **Administration:** This level deals with the day-to-day business operations of the firm, including personnel, finances, office services, and systems. Depending on the firm's size, a nonlawyer often serves as the administrator.
3. **Practice management:** This level holds responsibility for the management of lawyers and legal assistants, including the methods and systems used by them to deliver legal services to clients.

A law firm's success and stability depend in part on its professional organization. A law firm should continually evaluate how it is managed and operated and determine whether it meets the current needs of the entire firm. There is no "best" way to structure management. The appropriate structure is the one that works best at a given time in a firm's life.

A management structure that worked well when a firm had only five lawyers may not work when it is has twenty lawyers. Management structures must change with the firm's maturation, the personalities of the firm's members, and the growth or reduction of various areas of practice.

The structure that was effective during the first generation of a firm's life usually must change as the firm ages and new lawyers move into more responsible positions. In addition, modifications or changes may be needed to accommodate the ego of a superstar who strongly needs input into the firm. Branch office expansion may also require a management structure review.

The following sections describe the most common types of management structures found in small firms, along with the pros and cons of each structure. Keep in mind that, regardless of its organization, a firm's management structure will not be effective without effective leadership.

A BENEVOLENT DICTATOR OR STRONG MANAGING PARTNER

In the "benevolent dictator" system, one lawyer is selected to make almost all decisions regarding the management and operations of the law firm. Other lawyers have little or no input into how the firm operates. The person occupying this position usually does not have a term of office and is often a founding or more senior member of the firm. This type of structure was very common before the 1970s.

Pros

On the positive side, having a strong managing partner provides a very efficient system because only one lawyer's time is spent in management, permitting all other lawyers to practice law. Decisions are usually made and implemented quickly. Only one person needs to spend the time and effort to become familiar with how the firm operates. The nonlawyer administrator or manager has only one boss.

Cons

On the negative side, new leaders are usually not developed, creating a leadership and management vacuum upon the death or departure of the leader. Moreover, the lawyer assuming the position may not have the skills to do the job. In addition, this type of management often creates resentment when lawyers are not consulted or when they disagree with a decision or course of action. A great deal of mistrust in and lack of commitment to a firm can occur if the leader has values, philosophies, or goals that are different from those of the other lawyers. Today most lawyers want to be involved in management decisions that affect their professional career and their future. Firms with this type of management structure usually have a history of turnovers and split offs.

A MANAGEMENT OR EXECUTIVE COMMITTEE

A committee is a common form of management in firms with more than ten owners when there is not a natural leader or when no person wants to spend a significant amount of time in management. The firm's development stage determines how this committee is formed; what it does; where its authority and responsibility are; and whether it is elected, rotated, or self-perpetuating. The management or executive committee may establish or appoint subcommittees with responsibility for specific areas of management such as the library, associates, personnel, technology, and marketing. A firm that is large enough to have a management committee is usually large enough to need the services of a full-time administrator.

Pros

The management committee system requires more participatory management or the sharing of management responsibilities by a small group, especially if subcommittees are used. It keeps members involved and facilitates communication and a sense of belonging. In addition, it reduces the amount of time one lawyer would have to spend in managing. This structure can also be used to check the power or influence of a "key member" of the firm whom other members do not trust or to whom they are unwilling to give much authority.

Cons

On the other hand, this committee system requires more lawyer time, which is costly. Committees often do not perform as expected and are only effective if they have good leaders. This structure may create overlap or duplication of effort with other committees or the administrator. Lack of implementation is often a serious problem with this type of structure.

COMMITTEE OF THE WHOLE

With a "committee of the whole" system, usually all members of the firm—and at times all lawyers—are involved in all decisions that affect the firm. All members meet as a group on some predetermined schedule or whenever a decision needs to be made. This type of structure is common in firms with fewer than ten lawyers. However, some larger firms try to continue this type of governance beyond the time when it should be discontinued. This type of approach is often used when a firm becomes dissatisfied with a benevolent dictator.

Pros

On the plus side, rule by all fills the need that most lawyers have to be part of the decision-making process, especially when it comes to how their firms are run. It provides a sense of participation and facilitates internal communication by providing a flow of information regarding the firm's management.

Cons

Among the cons of this structure is that it is a very expensive method. It may lead to a great deal of talk but few or poor decisions because of the lack of understanding, knowledge, or background. Often decisions go unimplemented because no one has the requisite authority or responsibility. This form of consensus management often leads to paralysis or an inability to make difficult decisions. An administrator may not be very effective because of the lack of accountability and the overabundance of bosses.

A MANAGING PARTNER WITH A PRACTICE MANAGEMENT COMMITTEE

The pairing of a managing partner with a practice management committee is an emerging model in firms with more than ten lawyers. The managing partner is typically elected for a definite term, with sole responsibility for the firm's day-to-day management. He or she is usually assisted by an administrator who has the authority of a chief operating officer. The managing partner serves as chairperson of the practice management committee, which is comprised of representatives from each practice area or other members of the firm with authority and responsibility to manage the delivery of legal services. This committee often replaces a management or executive committee. The firm's size, maturity, and practice areas determine the committee's size, the way it is chosen, and the scope of its authority. The administrator is accountable to and often serves at the pleasure of the managing partner.

Pros

Having a managing partner who works in tandem with a practice management committee minimizes the amount of lawyer time spent on the firm's business operations. It focuses lawyer time on managing the delivery of legal services. It also provides for more accountability regarding work allocation, quality control, associates supervision, marketing, and planning. In addition, this structure involves lawyers in practice group activities and meetings, which fosters specialization, teamwork, sharing of work, and a sense of belonging.

Cons

On the negative side, this management structure requires that lawyers give up some autonomy regarding work acceptance and allocation, billing, use of associates, and other areas that directly affect the substantive production of legal work. It involves more lawyer time in managing the delivery of legal services, and it requires more accountability in the areas of marketing, planning, and management. Members of the practice management committee and practice group chairs may lack the required leadership skills.

ROLES AND RESPONSIBILITIES WITHIN THE FIRM

In many small and medium-sized firms, management is often ineffective and there is poor accountability because management roles and responsibilities have not been defined. In addition, many nonlawyer administrators or managers are often underutilized because of confusion or a lack of understanding regarding their function and authority. What are the responsibilities of the partners and management bodies within a law firm?

A Partner's Role

Defining the role of a partner is the first step to improving the governance, administration, and practice management of a law firm. In most small and medium-sized firms, partners have the responsibilities listed in Exhibit A.

The Managing Partner's or Management Committee's Role

After defining the role of a partner, the next step is to define the role of the managing partner, administrator, and any firm committees or practice groups.

Exhibit A.   Responsibilities of a Partner

> Adopt and amend the partnership agreement.
> Elect and remove partners.
> Merge, consolidate, reorganize, and dissolve the partnership.
> Make all decisions concerned with the death, disability, retirement, and withdrawal of partners.
> Make all major policy decisions, including but not limited to the following:
> 1. Areas of practice or specialization
> 2. Size of firm
> 3. Location of offices
> 4. Billing practices
> 5. Practice management
> Approve or disapprove the following:
> 1. Income, expense, and capital improvements budget
> 2. Major purchases exceeding predetermined amounts not authorized by the budget
> 3. Hiring of an administrator
> 4. Associate and clerkship employment and compensation
> Review and approve or disapprove any determinations of the managing partner, the management committee, or any other firm committees or groups.
> Approve or disapprove partner compensation.
> Elect the managing partner and members of the compensation committee.

In lieu of a managing partner, some small firms assign members of a management committee responsibility for certain areas of the firm's operations such as personnel, finance, equipment, technology, and facilities. When this variation is used, the administrator is accountable to each member of the committee. Exhibit B lists the authority and responsibilities often delegated to a managing partner or management committee.

Exhibit B.   Responsibilities of the Managing Partner or Management Committee

Determine and take appropriate action with respect to the following:
1. Compensation of nonlawyer personnel
2. Personnel policies for nonlawyer personnel
3. Expenditures authorized by firm budget
4. Office expansions and contractions
5. Contracts for consulting and professional services
6. Office assignments
7. Employment, evaluation, and discharge of the administrator, subject to approval of the partners
8. Interpretation of firm policies for the administrator
9. Bookkeeping, accounting, filing, control, conflict checking, retrieval of work product, and computer systems
10. Defining staff personnel positions
11. Insurance coverage
12. Organization of the staff
13. Employment and termination of legal assistants
14. Client and staff satisfaction
15. Compliance with federal, state, and local tax and employment laws.

Monitor and report to the partners with respect to the following:
1. Billings
2. Collections
3. Cash flow
4. Financial conditions and projections of the partnership
5. Performance of the administrator
6. General staff performance and morale

Make recommendations to the partners concerning the following:
1. Income, expense, cash flow, and capital budgets
2. Major office expenditures or leases over predetermined amounts not authorized by firm budgets
3. Office locations
4. Major office expansions and contractions
5. Creation or disbanding of firm committees
6. Delegation of authority to firm committees or practice groups
7. Firm policy
8. Strategic planning
9. Partner fringe benefits
10. Community and bar association activities

Fulfill such other responsibilities as are delegated by the partners from time to time.

Keep full and informative minutes of meetings and distribute them promptly to all partners.

The Administrator's Role

Many administrators are ineffective or have short tenures with a firm because the firm has not defined their role or the role of a partner, the managing partner, or the management committee.

Once the partners define and approve the administrator's duties and responsibilities, the firm is positioned to employ and use an administrator effectively. The skills and expertise that the administrator needs depend on the size of the firm, how much the firm is willing to pay, whether the firm has previously employed an administrator, and how much authority and responsibility he or she will be given.

The administrator's qualifications will vary by firm and depend greatly on the duties and responsibilities to be assumed. In most firms with fewer than ten lawyers, the administrator should be a hands-on person who will be involved in all aspects of the firm's day-to-day operations. In larger firms, the administrator may need assistance with personnel, finances, and other support services.

In small firms, personnel experience or "people skills" are essential qualifications for administrators. In addition, bookkeeping, budgeting, and other basic financial skills are very important, as is familiarity with technology. It is possible to supplement an administrator's lack of experience or expertise in the financial and technological areas with outside help. However, it is almost impossible to provide this type of assistance when an administrator has weak or poor personnel skills. When an administrator is not effective in personnel management, the managing partner or some other lawyer gets drawn into personnel management or there is no personnel management. Exhibit C sets out the responsibilities usually given an administrator in a small firm.

When looking for an administrator, a firm should consider doing the following:

- Place an advertisement in a local newspaper or in a larger newspaper in a city in the firm's geographic region.
- Contact the local chapter of the Association of Legal Administrators (ALA). If there is no local chapter in the area, the ALA's national headquarters, in Vernon Hills, Illinois, offers a service that puts firms in touch with administrators looking for employment.
- Advise administrators in other local firms that the firm is looking for an administrator.
- Hire a consultant or executive placement service.

The Practice Group's Role

Many firms are concluding that allowing lawyers complete autonomy in the delivery of legal services to clients is often not efficient and profitable. Furthermore, as firms grow and the practice of law becomes more complex and competitive, the traditional method of centralized management often creates an unworkable structure.

Exhibit C.   Responsibilities of the Administrator

Attend partner meetings and serve as an ex officio member of all firm committees, except for the compensation committee.

Serve as a resource person to firm committees and practice groups.

Assist the managing partner or other firm committees and practice groups in fulfilling their respective duties.

Maintain office manuals and records of the actions of the partners, practice groups, and firm committees, and furnish minutes of all such meetings to all partners.

Determine and take appropriate action with respect to the following:

1. Employment and discharge of all employees other than legal assistants, associates, and law clerks
2. Deployment, evaluation, and training of all employees other than legal assistants, associates, and law clerks
3. Specific personnel responsibilities include the following:
   a. Interviewing, screening, and hiring applicants for all office staff positions
   b. Evaluating the performance and contribution of office staff at least annually
   c. Counseling employees who are not meeting firm standards and telling them how to improve
   d. Taking disciplinary action against employees, including dismissal
   e. Being the spokesperson for lawyers in dealing with support staff
   f. Handling all staff-level personnel problems
   g. Maintaining up-to-date and comprehensive personnel records for each employee
   h. Training and developing support staff
   i. Having responsibility for communicating and enforcing firm policies and procedures
   j. Regulating work flow within the office for individual staff members
   k. Providing a staff that effectively supports the production of legal services
   l. Scheduling vacations for staff employees
   m. Developing programs for maintenance and improvement of employee morale
   n. Arranging for termination of employees who must leave for personal reasons or because of the inability to perform tasks assigned to them
   o. Maintaining and developing compliance programs required by state or federal law
   p. Developing job descriptions for all staff positions within the firm
   q. Assisting in outplacement of terminated associates, lawyers, and legal assistants
   r. Developing, publishing, and constantly updating office policy and procedures manuals concerned with the operations of the firm

Monitor and report to the managing partner or management committee with respect to the following:

1. Billings
2. Collections
3. Financial conditions and projections of the firm
4. Performance of employees, consultants, and independent contractors
5. General performance and morale of the staff

Manage the cash flow of the firm.

Exhibit C. Responsibilities of the Administrator (*continued*)

Plan, supervise, and be responsible for the following operations and systems:
1. Bookkeeping, accounting, and data processing
2. Billings and collections
3. Docket control and conflict checking
4. Information storage and retrieval
5. Word processing
6. Banking
7. Communication systems
8. Filing and records storage
9. Automated substantive legal systems

Plan and supervise the following:
1. Maintenance, repair, expansion, and contraction of all physical facilities
2. Acquisition, maintenance, repair, and disposition of furniture, fixtures, and equipment
3. Acquisition of resource materials and supplies
4. All nonlawyer personnel matters
5. Library operations

Prepare the following:
1. Proposed budgets
2. Statistical and partnership reports
3. Financial projections
4. Retirement or employee benefits reports to participants

Recommend and administer insurance programs and employee benefits.

Consult with individual lawyers and legal assistants with respect to the employment, deployment, training, evaluation, and discharge of the secretaries working for them.

Make recommendations to the managing partner or management committee with respect to the operations of the firm.

Stay current with law firm management practices.

Fulfill such other responsibilities as are delegated by the managing partner or management committee.

Delegate responsibility to assistants, with the consent of the managing partner or management committee.

Many managing partners or management committees become overburdened or are spread too thin. This malady is most acute in small firms with limited resources that have lawyers who must practice law *and* manage the firm.

Increasingly, some firms are decentralizing management authority by giving more responsibility and accountability to small practice groups, client teams, or marketing teams. These groups or teams are most effective when they are oriented toward a client, industry, or practice area and have the authority and responsibility to deal with most issues regarding the delivery of legal services.

Law firms must define the role of these groups and the role of those who manage them. Otherwise, the firm risks "creating firms within the firm" and encouraging the group to split off or leave the firm. Practice groups are often given the responsibilities listed in Exhibit D.

Exhibit D.   Responsibilities of Practice Groups

Develop forms, procedures, and a group precedent or work product retrieval system.

Approve and develop group continuing legal education programs.

Discuss workload and work assignments.

Develop and monitor quality control and service procedures.

Review existing library materials in the group's area of practice, recommend acquisitions, and eliminate materials and services not used or needed.

Monitor and discuss billing and collection matters.

Provide a forum for discussion of ethical standards related to the group's area of practice.

Make recommendations to the administrator concerning personnel needs and other support requirements.

Assist in the training, supervision, and evaluation of associates and legal assistants.

Determine tasks and responsibilities that can be delegated to legal assistants and other support staff.

Determine and implement business development and strategic plans, with the assistance of the managing partner or other designated partner or committee.

The Practice Group Chairperson's Role

Each practice group should be managed by a chairperson. How these persons should be chosen, how long they should serve, and what qualifications they should have depend on the size of the firm, the nature of its practice, and the abilities of its lawyers. A chairperson should have the responsibility to manage the affairs of the practice group as set out in Exhibit E.

The Practice Management Committee's Role

A firm's success and prosperity depend on effectively using, coordinating, and managing lawyer time in delivering legal services and developing business rather than leaving those decisions to the discretion of each lawyer. To avoid the risk of practice groups operating as "firms within the firm," the efforts and activities of these groups need to be coordinated on a firmwide basis by a practice management committee.

The practice management committee should be comprised of the managing partner (who should serve as chairperson) and representatives of the practice groups or other designated members of the firm. Members are usually appointed by the managing partner or elected by the partners. This type of committee is most effective when it has at least three and not more than five members. The practice management committee in small or medium-sized firms usually has the management duties and responsibilities listed in Exhibit F.

Exhibit E.   Responsibilities of the Practice Group Chairperson

> Establish practice group goals and objectives for each year, consistent with the firm's strategic plan.
>
> Ensure that the work of clients is promptly, responsibly, and competently completed and that services are economically performed, with the work being delegated to the most appropriate level.
>
> Allocate workload with a view to efficiency and the development of expertise in various substantive areas and ensure that all group members are meeting performance plans and firm goals.
>
> Monitor the supervision of professional, legal assistant, and support staff, coordinating the evaluation of and communication concerning individual performance and otherwise being attentive to staff morale.
>
> Ensure that the work undertaken is likely to be profitable and that fees are billed and collected in a timely manner.
>
> Devise and implement procedures to keep the professional staff regularly informed of what is happening in the firm and developments in the law, and make known and encourage specialized learning opportunities.
>
> Develop and maintain forms, systems, and procedures peculiar to the group, including file maintenance and client communications, and orient new personnel concerning them.
>
> Work with the administrator to ensure that satisfactory support staff and equipment are available and that staff are properly trained, supervised, and utilized.
>
> Ensure that all group members support and perform within firm policies and guidelines.
>
> Ensure that policies of the firm and group are implemented and enforced in coordination with the managing partner.
>
> Appoint such assistants as are necessary to help in managing and carrying out the responsibilities of the group.
>
> Consult with the compensation committee regarding compensation of partners in the group.
>
> Conduct evaluations of partners in the group.

Most lawyers believe in the concept of practice management, but many have difficulty making it work because of their unwillingness to give up some independence or to spend the time and effort to manage and work with others. It is also difficult to implement because many lawyers practice in more than one area or represent a number of clients with different needs. To achieve success in practice management, the firm needs to do the following:

- Appoint individuals who are good managers, who are committed to the concept of practice management, and who are willing to spend the required time. These individuals need not be the most senior people in the candidate pool.
- Have each practice group develop marketing and strategic plans that determine, among other things, how resources will be allocated, what services will be performed and who will perform them, what value pricing methods will be used, and how each lawyer's practice should be focused.

Exhibit F.   Responsibilities of the Practice Management Committee

---

Approve the following:

1. Practice group assignments for assistants and clerks
2. Fee schedules and major fee agreements

Recommend to the partners the following:

1. Creation of firm committees and chairperson assignments for them
2. Number of associates and clerks that should be hired
3. Compensation for associates, legal assistants, and clerks
4. Firm policy
5. Associates who should be considered for membership in the firm

Determine procedures for the intake and assignment of work.

Create an ongoing dialogue to make certain that cooperation and communication occur between the lawyers in each practice group.

Set standards for quality control and service, including issuing of opinion letters.

Establish training, supervision, and evaluation procedures for associates and legal assistants and coordinate those efforts on a firmwide basis.

Coordinate in-house and outside CLE programs.

Develop and coordinate performance plans for lawyers and legal assistants.

Coordinate the development of precedent or other firmwide retrieval systems.

Develop a lawyer policy and procedures manual.

Meet at regularly scheduled times pursuant to an agenda prepared by the managing partner, but not less than monthly.

Determine mentor assignments for associates and legal assistants and make certain that each of them is receiving regular and meaningful performance feedback.

Recommend business development and strategic plans to the partners.

Make all determinations regarding conflicts or matters arising under the Rules of Professional Conduct.

Authorize and conduct client assessment surveys.

- Use the practice groups as conduits for improved communication among management, lawyers, and support staff. Effective communication travels in two directions—from the top down and from the bottom up. In too many firms, without a practice management structure communication travels from the top down or not at all.
- Reward practice group leaders when their group meets performance goals or is effective. By the same token, there should be some penalty when they fail to provide leadership or their group does not meet goals or objectives.
- Have practice group leaders meet regularly to discuss all issues relevant to the firm's delivery of legal services (e.g., work allocation, marketing, and professional personnel needs). These meetings or the supervision by the practice management committee should not result in micromanaging of the groups.

- Include practice group leaders in compensation deliberations.

Depending on the size and resources of the firm, special committees may be created for marketing, recruiting, strategic planning, and compensation purposes.

COMMON MANAGEMENT PROBLEMS IN SMALL AND MEDIUM-SIZED FIRMS

Finally, firms must be ever vigilant to the problems that can occur with any management structure. Here are twenty-eight common problems against which firms should guard.

1. Recruitment into management of lawyers who have no interest or skills or are not willing to spend the time required.
2. Unwillingness to give compensation credit or reward to those who serve in management positions.
3. Administrators who have no authority or responsibility or who have to be told everything to do.
4. Too much emphasis on financial matters and not enough time or effort devoted to personnel issues and concerns.
5. Lack of annual goals or objectives for the firm, its managers, or practice groups.
6. Failure to define in writing the role of the partners, managing partner, administrator, and practice groups.
7. Too much lawyer time spent on business operations and not enough on practice management matters.
8. Too many partner meetings devoted to trivial matters and too few partner meetings devoted to practice management issues, including planning and marketing.
9. Too many meetings devoted to financial matters or expenditure of funds, which would not be necessary if the firm had a budget.
10. Lawyers who want to micromanage.
11. Lawyers who cannot or will not delegate.
12. Administrators who cannot or will not delegate.
13. Lack of a policy and procedures manual or having a manual that is out-of-date.
14. The effort to make all decisions by consensus.
15. Lack of communication between (a) the managing partner and partners, (b) the managing partner and administrator, (c) the administrator and staff, (d) partners and associates, or (e) lawyers and assigned support staff.
16. Crises or reactive management philosophy.
17. Failure to consult with those who will be affected by a decision before the decision is made.
18. "Empire building" by administrators.
19. Recruitment into management of a partner who is near retirement.

20. Inability to make change in management because no term of office exists for managers.
21. Lack of information regarding what the managers do at both the lawyer and staff levels.
22. Lack of implementation of partner decisions or of firm policies and procedures.
23. Failure to define the roles and responsibilities of key administrative staff.
24. A managing partner who fails to sell the administrator to partners and staff.
25. Neglect of or lack of appreciation for the firm's employees.
26. Failure to evaluate the administrator's performance annually.
27. Unwillingness to send the administrator or managing partner to law office management seminars or conferences.
28. An administrator or managing partner who is satisfied with the status quo or who does not want to "rock the boat."

Successful law firms recognize that the practice of law is both a profession and a business. Law firms that choose the proper management structure reduce conflict within the firm, project a desirable image to clients and lawyers outside of the firm, and make the practice of law more profitable and enjoyable.

CHAPTER 5

Two-Tiered Partnerships

Bruce D. Heintz

This chapter describes the appropriate use of a two-tiered partnership. For firms with such a structure already in place, the chapter may provide ideas for modifications and enhancements.

At the outset, it should be noted that the subject of two-tiered partnerships is a controversial one. Many firms have such organizations—some are happy with the results and others are in angst. A firm's management must weigh the potential benefits and drawbacks of a two-tiered partnership and be prepared for the extra effort required to implement one effectively and in a way that maintains morale.

An additional caveat: Restructuring a law firm raises many *legal* questions. Be certain to consult a business lawyer on these.

THE RISE OF TWO-TIERED PARTNERSHIPS

Two-tiered partnerships in law firms are not new. Many firms, notably in the Midwest, have operated such partnerships for decades. Traditionally, in these partnerships a new associate was admitted to the "second tier," which was a nonequity, essentially "contract employee" position. This second-tier or "junior partner" rank gave the firms a few additional years to evaluate candidates' performances before deciding whether to make them full partners.

However, with the advent of the roaring 1980s for the legal profession, a new use of two-tiered partnerships arose. Many single-tiered equity firms, finding that they had overhired associates in the late 1970s and early 1980s, now faced enormous demographic bulges of associates knocking at the partnership doors in the mid- to late-1980s, particularly as the overall growth in the firms slowed. At this time much debate within firm management centered on "dilution of equity," "can we afford all these partners," and similar concerns. Yet on the other side of the argument, partners exclaimed, "We made a commitment to these young associates when we hired them. We can't just turn them out now." In addition, the thought leaders in the profession were saying that it seemed wasteful to train such good talent, and then just get rid of it under the old "up or out" policies. Further, some firms felt that they already had, de facto, two tiers of partners: those who brought in the clients (and worked themselves very hard) and those who either were not able to do this or felt that lifestyle was more important. The situation was ripe for a compromise: the two-tiered partnership.

By now, two-tiered partnerships have become commonplace. At least one-fourth or more of all firms have two-tiered partnerships. Most that have them are quite pleased with the added flexibility and opportunity provided, both for the firm and for the second-tier partners. Yet, of course, some aspects of these partnerships are still problematical.

For research in preparing this chapter, interviews were conducted with managing partners of twelve law firms with two-tiered partnerships, ranging from smaller and medium-sized firms to several large firms, located around the country. These managing partners were generally quite enthusiastic about the benefits, particularly the benefit of "flexibility" that their firms have derived from their two-tiered partnerships. Some respondents, however, warned of some troublesome aspects of two-tiered partnerships and situations when such an approach to structuring the firm was not appropriate. Both sides of this issue are discussed in the following sections.

KEY DIFFERENCES AND NOMENCLATURE FOR THE TWO LEVELS

Terminology varies among firms and can be a bit confusing. The key difference between the tiers is that "first-tier" partners are true equity holders in the firm or corporation. Accordingly, they have to pay in capital, must assume a portion of the firm's liabilities, can vote on important matters such as partner admissions or management elections, are entitled to "split up the pie" (divide firm distributable income), and are usually entitled to some buyback of their ownership interests when they retire. Alternative nomenclature for these partners is: equity partners, full partners, ("just plain") partners, senior partners (but not referring to age or long tenure with the firm), ownership members, and shareholders.

The "second-tier" partners are, legally, salaried employees, not owners. They do not contribute capital and assume none of the firm's general liabilities (yet in some cases, such arrangements have been structured, if only in a "phantom" way). While they do not have the legal authority to vote on many matters (e.g., the compensation of the first-tier partners), often firms will allow second-tier partners to participate in management and policy setting, such as voting in the elections for managing partner. The primary difference between the tiers, however, is that the second-tier partners are employees whose compensation is set by the firm (as opposed to dividing up distributable net income, as the owners do).

Of course, many compensation alternatives are used in addition to straight salary, such as incentive bonuses based both on the second-tier partner's performance and how good a year it was for the firm. Alternative nomenclature for these partners is: salaried partners, income partners, junior partners (although this appellation is becoming rarer, possibly because of its connotations), "B" or plan "B" partners, nonequity partners, and contract shareholders.

ADVANTAGES OF A TWO-TIERED PARTNERSHIP

Firms with two-tiered partnerships variously list the advantages as follows:

- Provides an additional window of time to review associates' performance and to decide whether they should be admitted to full (or equity) partnership
- Offers the possibility of earlier entry point (i.e., with fewer years with the firm) for associates on the way to full partnership
- Allows firms to retain persons with solid and valuable skills who might otherwise have to leave the firm if they were not promoted to full partner
- Provides a position for those who need alternative work-style arrangements (e.g., part-time)
- Provides a temporary holding position for new lateral partners, giving the firm a chance to consider their fit for a year or two before admission to the equity partnership
- May add to clients' perceptions that they are getting high-level attention and may be advantageous for business development purposes because more persons hold the title of "partner" (although these advantages are debated by some observers)
- Provides a position to which the firm can "demote" full partners if their performance has decreased (as an alternative to being asked to leave the firm)
- Provides a transition position for retiring partners
- Supports associates' psychological needs to be upwardly mobile in their organization when they are not yet ready to be a full partner
- Offers more attractive opportunities for associates and therefore better recruiting results

DISADVANTAGES OF A TWO-TIERED PARTNERSHIP

Firms with two-tiered partnerships variously list the disadvantages as follows:

- Provides a position for persons who are, in reality, performing below the firm's standards for tenure and who, if the firm applied its standards with more courage, should really be asked to leave (i.e., up or out)

- May become a position for women with part-time needs and/or minorities, as a way to avoid the issues of firm need, competency, and prejudice
- Can cause resentment amongst the second tier if first-tier partners are not visibly more productive, do not produce more business, and are not otherwise demonstrably more valuable and "worth" their full partner status
- Can reduce the added motivation and productivity that may result from an associate knowing that he or she will face an up or out decision in a specified time period
- Can siphon off types of work that would otherwise be used for training associates coming up the ranks
- May be a way of avoiding the real issue of who should be promoted, if used merely as a compromise decision to deal with a demographic bulge of associates ready for promotion
- Can cause poor morale in the second-tier group based on feelings of "second-class citizenship"
- Causes more complications with respect to firm management functions (e.g., do second-tier partners attend normal partner meetings and events, and in what other ways are they to be treated like associates rather than partners?)
- May allow persons to represent themselves to clients and the public as "partners" when the firm may not be comfortable with that representation
- May have an adverse impact on recruiting if associates perceive that the existence of a second tier means that there are fewer opportunities for promotion to first tier

STRUCTURE OF A TWO-TIERED PARTNERSHIP

There are several primary forms and many variants to the design of two-tiered partnership structures in law firms. Some of the usual approaches and design options are explained here.

Junior Partners/Senior Partners

This structure is, for the most part, a modification of the traditional "up or out" partnership structure. The expectation here is that within a specified time period (e.g., three or four years) all persons admitted to the junior position will be judged as worthy of promotion to senior partner. Those not granted a promotion to senior partner are asked to leave the firm after the three- or four-year "probationary period" in the junior partner slot.

Obviously, this approach enhances the up-or-out form of partnership with a mechanism for viewing candidates for partnership that allows them to operate with somewhat more responsibility than associates. In addition, both the full partners and the newly promoted salaried partners know that the candidates are being closely watched for potential promotion to equity partner. In firms operating with this structure, entry into the junior classification may be possible at an earlier point in an associate's career than entry into the senior position would be if the senior position were all that were offered. This can be useful to the firm in recruiting and motivating associates.

Equity Partners/Income Partners

This is the most common form of the two-tiered approaches. The key feature here is that once promoted to the income partner level, persons can stay in that role indefinitely, or at least as long as their performance supports their tenure. (The roles and responsibilities of equity versus income partners and the requirements for promotion are discussed later.)

In many firms, it is expected that some or many of the income partners will remain in that role for their entire careers with the firm. This structure provides a "tenured" position with organizational status (e.g., a "partner") to persons who are expected to perform high-quality work at a significant level of output, but who are not necessarily responsible for being rainmakers or carrying some of the other responsibilities of an owner.

Of course, like the senior partner/junior partner model described previously, some of the income partners are expected to grow to assume greater responsibilities and to be promoted later to equity partner. Income partner is not the end of the line at all; in organizationally healthy firms, the equity partners do all they can to train and encourage income partners to progress.

The ratio of equity partners to income partners varies greatly among firms. Some have more income partners than equity partners, up to one and one-half times as many. In other firms, the number of incumbents in the income partner position is modest, perhaps only one-fourth as many members as in the equity category. Some firms have only a few incumbents. Several reasons are behind the differences in these ratios. For instance, in some firms, the income position is relatively new, and hence only a limited number of persons have been promoted into it. Other firms consciously attempt to keep the number in the income category to a minimum, just enough to handle those "special" cases of associates who are not ready for equity partnership but are too valuable, and have too much potential, to let go.

In most of the equity partner/income partner structures, associates are promoted first to the income tier and later, if they are eligible, to the equity tier. Some firms, however, promote qualified associates directly to the equity tier, allowing them to bypass the income category. Generally this strategy is only for exceptional candidates, providing an extra reward for qualified individuals.

Other Variants

Of course, there are other structures or adaptations in law firms that might be referred to as "two-tiered" partnerships.

One variant includes the use of "senior associates" or "career associates," in conjunction with a single, equity-tiered partnership. In these cases, there is no income class of partners but rather an upgraded position for associates. This senior associate position functions like a two-tiered partnership in that it enables the firm to retain persons who are valuable but not eligible for full partnership. Generally, this senior associate position is used only for a very few candidates with particular specialty skills, but not for persons who handle clients, supervise others, or develop business.

In another variant of the two-tiered approach, only a few partners hold all the equity, while the great majority of other partners function as income partners. This approach is relatively rare, but it may occur when a few entrepreneurial partners start a firm, develop all the business, and need only "worker" partners to conduct it. A very successful firm in the Northeast with more than thirty workers' compensation lawyers and sixteen "partners" is actually owned by only three of them. These three have put up all of the capital, are responsible for all of the liabilities and debt, and, in the good years, make significant profits.

Use of the Compensation Structure to Create Two Tiers

Some firms have chosen to create some of the benefits of a two-tiered partnership without actually establishing a nonequity position. This approach has been adopted in a number of firms that recognized that their partnership, de facto, operated in two tiers (i.e., the business developers/managers and the "worker" partners). In these cases, it was felt that creating a new nonequity position and then demoting many partners to it would be too organizationally explosive.

The alternative, then, is to develop a compensation system that mimics a two-tiered partnership. In these cases, the "second-tier" partners are paid a "base salary" with incentives for billed hours and new work brought in. After paying the second tier, the remainder is then divided among the first tier. Hence, in a poor economic year, the second-tier partners' incomes are somewhat protected on the downside, and in a good year, the first-tier partners gain the benefit of the upside.

Timing

Typically, new partners are admitted to the income class after four to eight years as an associate. A partner who later becomes eligible for full partnership usually earns that right within another two to four years. As mentioned before, however, some incumbents may remain in the income tier for an extended period of time, or for their entire careers.

DIFFERENCES IN THE RIGHTS AND RESPONSIBILITIES OF THE TWO TIERS

Some additional elaboration of the rights and responsibilities of the two tiers may be useful.

- **Capital:** Equity partners pay in capital (which is returned when the partner leaves or retires). Income partners do not.

- **Voting:** The firm's partnership agreement or corporate documents (e.g., shareholders' agreement, bylaws) should spell out for which items an "equity partner" vote is required and what margins the vote must achieve to carry. Typically, income partners do not have any legally granted voting rights, but many firms provide that these partners do participate and vote on a number of issues (e.g., election of a managing partner or other officials, changes to certain office policies).

- **Liabilities including debts:** Some income partners are pleased that they do not have these "rights," since it has become clear in recent years that a law firm's debts and other liabilities can be substantial. However, some firms have structured their second tier to assume some of the firm's liabilities. A notable example is the collapse of a major Boston law firm that left newly promoted income partners with several hundred thousand dollars of new personal liabilities.

- **Buyback of ownership interest and retirement:** When equity partners leave, and almost always when they retire, typically some payments are made to compensate for their "ownership" in the business. "Goodwill" is not recognized in law firms. However, absent an agreement to the contrary, a departing equity owner certainly has claim to some value in the receivables and other liquid assets of the firm (and in some cases, fixed assets like furniture and computer systems, but these are usually heavily depreciated). Income partners have no such claim. In fact, retirement approaches for income partners are typically nonexistent, or only beginning to be addressed, because of the newness of the position in many firms and the general lack of excess cash flow to fund retirements.

- **Employment contract:** Frequently the income partners have an employment contract that provides basic, but often minimal, rights. These contracts usually address compensation along with conditions of termination and severance pay. One managing partner interviewed mentioned that his firm's employment contract for the income tier was a one-year agreement, only renewable by the firm. This, he reports, makes it easy for the firm to part with nonperformers simply by not renewing the contract.

"PERFORMANCE" DIFFERENCES AND PROMOTION CRITERIA

The issues of performance differences and promotion criteria are key to a two-tiered partnership. Generally speaking, the equity tier is meant to include those partners who are business developers or who otherwise manage or control significant amounts of client business, and the income tier is meant for "worker" partners whose primary responsibility is to work on client matters. How these two definitions are interpreted or, even more important, how they are put into practice varies widely from firm to firm. Some operational definitions are provided in Exhibit A.

An extensive discussion of promotion criteria for partnerships is beyond the scope of this chapter. However, some advice regarding the promotion to equity partner includes: (1) keep it a subjective decision of the equity partnership, but use as much quantitative data as possible in making the decision; (2) put the criteria in writing and have discussions with associates to elaborate on the meaning of the criteria; and (3) point to partners in the firm who may serve as models for the ways partners can contribute, and hence as models of how the promotion criteria translate into decisions.

Also, it should be noted the several firms with formula systems for partnership compensation have attempted to establish quantitative standards for promotion to the equity level. In one such firm, for example, candidates for equity partnership who are currently income partners "must have numeric results, if the equity partner formula is applied, that place them above the lower quarter of existing equity partners." Firms using this approach report that while it has strong logical appeal, in practice it has been too

Exhibit A.   Definitions of Equity Partner and Income Partner

Equity Partner	Income Partner
Rainmaker or otherwise responsible for major business development, either firmwide or for a major practice	Contributing to business development is encouraged, but not expected; primary responsibility is to perform quality work at a high level of output
Member of a high-leverage practice or very visible lower leverage practice	Member of low-leverage practice or less visible one
Head of a practice or regularly manages income partners or a group of lawyers	Can and often works as a solo, yet also supervises associates
Actively participates in setting firm management policy and may serve in a management role, e.g., managing partner or on the executive committee	Expected to contribute to firm administration and participates on committees, but is not eligible for high-level management positions

high a hurdle for income partners to jump over, owing to the high value placed on business origination within the equity partner compensation formula.

DETERMINING COMPENSATION

Typically, an income partner has a guaranteed base salary (e.g., $110,000 per year). On top of this, most firms offer the opportunity for some sort of incentive bonus or "share" of profits if the firm's year is successful. For example, often a simple bonus arrangement is offered, providing for payments of up to 20 percent of an income partner's base salary, if the partner's performance is excellent. Usually the amount of this bonus is determined subjectively by a compensation committee of equity partners. In some firms that employ a formula compensation system, however, these incentive bonuses are based on quantitative approaches (e.g., a direct calculation of the payment based on the dollar value of the partner's collected hours). When subjectivity is involved, often compensation committees also take into account how good a year it was for the firm when deciding the size of bonus to award each income partner. In some firms, the size of the bonuses to income partners is calculated based on the level of firm profits: for example, a bonus pool is created for income partners to the extent that firm profits exceed a certain predefined level.

Compensation for equity partners is often no different for two-tiered firms than for single-tiered firms. However, what is left to split up as distributable income is the net of the compensation payments made to the income partners.

As mentioned previously, a primary benefit of the two-tiered approach is that the income partners' take-home pay is somewhat protected on the downside in poor economic years (yet limited on the upside in good years), while the equity partners receive the benefits (or pains) of the swings in profitability from year to year. (In the recent economically volatile years there have been many income partners who were glad to be sheltered in the relative protection of that category, and not a few equity partners who, probably only half jokingly, wished they were income partners.)

HOW IT FEELS TO BE A "SECOND-TIER" PARTNER

This is one of the potentially troublesome aspects of a two-tiered partnership. While in theory the structure is intended to give status and meaning to "another role" in the firm, sometimes things do not work out so well in practice.

Many incumbents in the income partner group seem to suffer from "second-class citizen" feelings. These feelings can be rooted in the actual structure of the income partnership (e.g., not enough voting rights are granted), the way equity partners "treat" them, or income partners' own internal assessments of whether they "have a good deal" or "feel valued."

The first and most effective way to minimize these difficulties is to ensure that the difference between first-tier and second-tier partners is perceptibly different. Income partners chafe at seeing equity partners who are not working hard yet seem to be enjoying the benefits of "merely having been admitted at an earlier stage in the firm's growth." When the responsibilities and pressures felt by the equity partners are more obvious (e.g., constant anxiety over developing new business), income partners are more likely to accept the differences in incomes and status between the two groups.

A second way to deal with second-class citizenship problems is to ensure that the implied "messages" given by the equity partners about the income partners' worth are positive. A "how to" list for creating a constructive atmosphere for income partners should include the following points:

- Respect from and inclusion by the equity partners. This can be translated into many example behaviors and the appropriate language that equity partners should employ when working with income partners.
- Inclusion in firm meetings. The few exceptions would involve "equity decisions" (e.g., equity partner admissions and compensation, a major merger).
- Informal involvement in all major policy issues of the firm. An effective managing partner will make sure income partners participate in discussions leading up to any major changes in the firm and all changes that significantly affect the income partners.
- Access to resources, such as secretarial support, and consideration when it comes to office size. While cost control is very important, one of the things that seems to roil second-tier partners the most is receiving "second-class" support with respect to secretaries, tools, working conditions, and office size. The level of support provided to income partners should probably not be the same as that required for equity partners; however, the point is that equity partners need to be sensitive to the perspective of income partners on this subject.

A second major trouble point for the income tier is the question, "How do I get promoted to equity partner?" This, of course, is not a new question, but has taken on new proportions in some firms. The firms that established their two-tiered partnerships in response to the projected demographic bulges of associates coming up for partnership face this question on a grand scale. For many of these firms, the decision regarding these large groups of associates was merely delayed while the firm "bought some time" by offering the new second-tier position. These firms now again face a "demographic bulge" as the income partners, who have been in that position for four or five years, are now asking, "Is it time, yet?" The painful answer will have to lie in admitting some, but not all, of these heretofore "peers" into the firm's equity partnership and asking others to leave.

Finally, with respect to the happiness of those in the second tier, some income partners do take real solace in the fact that, if it were not for the existence of the second tier, they would probably have been forced to leave the firm.

RISK OF EASING PARTNERSHIP STANDARDS AND ADMITTING MARGINAL CANDIDATES

In the interviews, managing partners mentioned easing partnership standards as a potential pitfall to avoid. However, some firms have not been able to avoid it and are now having to deal with weak decisions made in the past.

Essentially, these firms took an attitude of "we don't have to be too discriminating on admissions to the income level because we have a second chance at making a discriminating decision when the candidates are up for full partner." Based on this lax attitude, some firms feel that a number of the lawyers admitted to the second tier should not have been added to any tier in the firm (i.e., they should have been "upped or outted"). Lax in not turning away candidates from the income tier in the first place, these firms now often do not have the organizational courage to admit their mistakes and ask some of those income partners to leave. One firm admits that the overall quality of the law firm was hurt by the retention of persons in the second tier who should have been weeded out earlier.

Firms that seem to have suffered the least from this condition boast that they established high standards for admission to the income class of partnership (and to the equity level also) and have not shied away from identifying persons who should be outplaced. Several managing partners experienced with two-tiered partnerships warned against making admission decisions to accommodate an individual's lifestyle choices. Keeping the firm's standard for high productivity is more important, they argue.

DEMOTING ESTABLISHED EQUITY PARTNERS TO THE SECOND TIER

Demoting established equity partners is theoretically possible, but many managing partners shudder at the thought of implementing it. The organizational adjustment and the stigma attached to a partner shifted from equity to income status is significant.

In a number of firms where it has been accomplished, however, the managing partners reported that their two-tiered structure provided opportunities for the firm, and the partner in question, that would not have been available before. In one case, a partner who wished to reduce his workload volunteered to enter the income tier to reduce his responsibilities, along with an agreed-to reduction in his compensation. In another case, the partner, who had been with the firm for many years and still provided a solid contribution, appreciated the opportunity to join the income tier instead of leaving the firm, as did several of his peers during a downsizing process at the firm.

USEFULNESS OF INCOME TIER FOR LATERAL HIRES

The income tier provides a useful "holding pattern" for new laterals who have joined the firm. In practice, many firms request that laterals remain as salaried partners for one to two years while the firm has a chance to "see them in action" and let the partners "get used to them." While a separate contract spelling out compensation based on production often places these new laterals on a different compensation basis than existing "normal" second-tier partners, for a firm where a two-tiered partnership already exists, the basic contractual and organizational structures for this arrangement are already conveniently in place.

OTHER BENEFITS A TWO-TIERED PARTNERSHIP STRUCTURE MIGHT PROVIDE

The managing partners interviewed for this chapter mentioned several other ways that their multitiered structures assisted their firms. One mentioned that the most significant effect of instituting the two-tiered structure was to control compensation in a way that paid adequately for the income partners (i.e., "not so little that they left, but better than they could get on the street"), while still leaving larger amounts of money to be divided up among the equity partners. Another managing partner mentioned that, in addition to allowing the firm to take a look at potential equity partners' performance, the position also allowed the current equity partners to "socialize" more with the candidates to get a better feel for their fit with firm culture and whether they would enjoy working with the candidates. Another managing partner suggested that her firm's two-tiered structure has helped them avoid conflicts over the potential promotion of a candidate "favored" by one or a few partners, but not generally supported by the entire equity partnership; in this case, promotion of the candidate into the income category was seen as the right answer by everyone, including the candidate.

ADDITIONAL LIABILITY CONSIDERATIONS

Clearly, as a matter of law, a second-tier partner may become liable to third parties by reason of being held out to persons outside the firm as "a partner." This occurrence, which could have significant financial impact, may be as simple as introducing a second-tier partner to a client, or even at a social function, as "my partner, Bill." In another example, a second-tier person's name on the letterhead, without being distinguished from the full partners' names, can also imply "full" partnership status, with all the rights (and in this case, all the liabilities) of that position.

A practice being adopted by many law firms is no longer to refer to their partners *of any tier* as "partners." Everyone in the firm is referred to as a "member," both outside and inside of the firm. While introducing someone as "my fellow member, Bill" needs a bit more polish before it will sound right, this appears to be a desirable practice.

On the other hand, a law firm may become liable to a second-tiered member for wrongful discharge or for other remedies available to employees that are not available to partners. As a matter of law, the second-tier partner has none of the attributes of a "partner" and all of the attributes of an "employee."

Liability in partnerships, as mentioned earlier, is a subject that is evolving dramatically. For example, a recent court case ruled that a "full" partner in one of the international accounting firms could actually be considered an "employee," because he had few of the normal powers of a partner (the firm is so large, while his portion of ownership and voice in management were so small). He therefore sued and won a sizable judgment for an alleged age-discriminatory layoff.

Some of this evolution relating to liabilities in law firms, to be defined both by lawmakers and the courts, will surely affect two-tiered partnerships. Hence, the caveat offered early in this chapter is repeated here: It is essential to take great care in reviewing applicable local statutes, bar rules, and active legal proceedings before designing a two-tiered partnership.

WHEN A TWO-TIERED PARTNERSHIP STRUCTURE IS NOT APPROPRIATE

As explained in earlier sections, two-tiered partnerships do not operate trouble-free. In many cases, in fact, a two-tiered partnership is not the right structure for a law firm. Some firms that have instituted such structures have encountered major difficulties that have become significant stumbling blocks against future firm success.

For one thing, some, or many, law firms simply may not need a two-tiered structure. Some firms may be too small (e.g., firms with ten or fewer lawyers) to make a two-tiered structure beneficial. Also, firms of any size that have a high leverage and a growing practice can operate quite successfully on the principle of up or out. This approach yields a highly competitive environment where the firm benefits by promoting only the few best associates who have proven themselves superior. In fact, to have a two-tiered structure in this case would be harmful because second-tier partners would be performing the work that formerly had been used as a "training ground" for associates coming up the line.

Further, many firms have established a two-tiered structure in reaction to a "demographic bulge" of associates approaching partnership in a firm where the growth had subsided. This precondition may not exist in every firm.

An important consideration for many lawyers and firms is that the concept of having more than one class of partners (i.e., "citizens") is philosophically abhorrent. Some firms that have instituted two-tiered partnerships without understanding the strength of their firm members' underlying feelings and attitudes about "classes of citizenship" have later regretted the decision.

Also, as many of the managing partners who were surveyed for this chapter reported, a two-tiered partnership is not for the weak of heart when it comes to telling a promotional candidate, "No." The second tier can create a major pitfall for firms that cannot say no by burdening them with less than qualified individuals as partners, even if they are second-tier partners.

Finally, even in the firms where a two-tiered partnership is reportedly "working," everyone must cope with the psychological dissonance of "we're all *partners*," yet "you are a different kind of partner than me." That is, the problems of second-class citizenry never seem to vanish altogether, even in the best of situations. Not everyone wants this kind of atmosphere around their firm on a daily basis.

CHAPTER 6

Compensation Systems for Law Firm Owners

James Cotterman, Dan DiLucchio, Thomas Clay, Ward Bower, and Peter Giuliani*

Devising a compensation program for law firm owners is by far the most difficult compensation topic.[1] One reason is that there is no perfect system. Compensation programs must fit the organization—its culture, its practice, and its clients. Different systems work well for different law firms. In addition, owners must deal from inside the circle on this issue. It is the compensation for risks taken, the confusion over the separation of the "arm's-length" value for an owner's labor, and the division of profits earned by the enterprise in general that create such controversy. This is an issue peculiar to closely held businesses, where the owners are active in the business's day-to-day affairs. In a manufacturing setting, there is much guidance on the relationships between the value for work rendered and the return on ownership. In a law firm, however, there is no such guidance.

The restructuring of the legal profession has brought many law firms to the realization that effective compensation systems must become active management tools. Law firms use compensation as the means to direct individuals' efforts toward the attainment of the organization's strategic mission. The competitive legal market has given clients a new voice in everything from staffing to pricing. Clients even evaluate lawyers on how closely the law firm's value systems align with their own.

This manuscript was prepared by Altman Weil Pensa, Inc. Contributions to the materials were made by James Cotterman, Dan DiLucchio, Thomas Clay, Ward Bower, and Peter Giuliani. Thanks to Diane Quinn for the transcription and proofreading of the text.

1. The form of organization selected by a law firm has significant impact on the tax consequences of its compensation system. It is largely irrelevant, however, when it comes to the principles used to decide compensation within a law firm. For purposes of this chapter, salary and draw are interchangeable terms, as are bonus and distribution.

Documentation differences, on the other hand, are very important because of the need to ensure the desired tax consequence of these transactions. Differences in compensation methodology between partnerships and professional corporations are, therefore, primarily driven by the tax treatments the firms and their owners receive.

It is important to note that such changes are like the tides—they come in and they go out. In a free market economy, there is a natural desire to reach equilibrium. Equilibrium is not reached as inertia takes the pendulum past dead center and toward the other extreme. Therefore, it is certainly possible that conditions will change in the future. The end of the 1980s and the beginning of the 1990s pushed the pendulum swing in a new direction.

THE ADVENT OF MERIT-BASED SYSTEMS

To cope with changing conditions, law firms have focused on the motivational aspect of compensation, moving their compensation programs toward objective merit-based systems that are integrated with individual goal setting and performance review programs. Static compensation systems are giving ground to more consciously managed systems that are based on a combination of both subjective and objective observations.

The migration toward managed systems for compensation has occurred gradually over the past decade. Lockstep and formula systems alike, while they retain their basic philosophies, have been modified to allow for more deliberate compensation decisions. Movement up the lockstep ladder each year is no longer guaranteed, and some individuals are being held or adjusted downward. Formula-driven systems have become less rigid with the introduction of "bonus pools" and other devices that allow law firms to adjust for the aberrations that formulas inevitably create.

In addition, law firms realize that effective compensation systems are not substitutes for good economic performance. A good compensation system cannot satisfy participants if the firm's economic results are poor. Conversely, a poor reward system can wreak havoc in even the most profitable firm. A firm must have both good economic performance *and* an effective reward system to maintain owner satisfaction.

The new merit-based systems require that law firms develop a clear statement of the subjective and objective measures of performance. Law firms blend subjective components with objective measurable criteria in their managed systems. In each case the criteria are consistent with the organization's strategic goals and client needs. Criteria, including the means and timing of measurement, must be well communicated for these systems to be effective.

Finding the right compensation system for a law firm is a function of understanding the people, the organization, and the practice that the system will cover. Each firm has its own personality, culture, and practice orientation. To succeed, the compensation system must be perceived as fair by those who are affected by it. To survive long term, the compensation program must be capable of change as the firm's needs change over time.

TRADITIONAL FORMULAS

Today there are many law firms in which the owners cannot agree to a value system. The typical response is to search for a formula that divides the profits fairly as to each partner's contribution. All too often, these formulas focus on the short-term history of what has happened (fees collected by various measures—personal, billing, originating), while ignoring those actions that build future value. Such programs diminish the concept of firm or institutional value. They foster an individual profit-center mentality (often referred to as "eat what you kill") that results in a self-centered practice rather than a firm-centered or client-centered organization.

Traditional compensation systems deserve a quick mention. There are four basic systems, with unlimited variations. The systems, in order of their historical roots, are as follows:

Static systems: These systems encompass seniority/lockstep, percentages/points, and equal sharing systems. They are built on traditional "apprentice to master" concepts that expect that individuals will learn their craft and slowly the rewards will come as they approach mastery. The foundational element, that longer service translates into greater value, just does not work in all cases.

Formulaic systems: These systems look at quantifiable economic factors, including, but not limited to, billable hours, fees collected, matters managed, and clients developed. They typically foster very independent views of what a law firm means. The result is often a group of space sharers with independent practices rather than a law firm.

Subjective or institutional systems: These systems attempt to identify the "total contribution" of an individual by looking at a variety of objective and subjective information regarding the individual's performance. They are an improvement over pure formulaic systems, although they suffer many of the same problems. However, they often fail to measure what clients value and are overly focused on the short term.

Traditional or combined systems: These systems mix the subjective or institutional system and the seniority/lockstep system, blending seniority and formulaic and subjective factors to measure contribution to the law firm. They represent an attempt to blend what people like most from other systems. They too suffer from a short-term focus and lack of client value integration.

The following sections describe the various subjective and objective measurements that law firms consider in their compensation decisions. Not all criteria are used, nor are they used in similar fashions from law firm to law firm. Interestingly, one might expect that small law firms would overwhelmingly implement subjective, participative systems that accommodate the general decision-making style and their familiarity with each other's contributions. Likewise, one would expect that large firms would tend toward less personal systems like formulas because significant size makes intimate knowledge of each partner's contributions more difficult. However, that premise is not the case. Twenty-three percent of law firms with fewer than twenty lawyers elect formulaic systems while only 14 percent of law firms with one hundred or more lawyers use formulas, according to a 1993 Altman Weil Pensa survey.[2] Large law firms understand that it is very difficult to sustain size if the institution does not have value. Therefore, the large firms generally look toward more "institutionalized" approaches to compensation. Smaller firms have less at stake in terms of institutional identity and often value the rugged independence that small firm practice affords. Formula systems therefore have less downside risk in those instances.

SUBJECTIVE CRITERIA

Subjective considerations in compensation systems should cover the attributes of good, productive lawyers. Many, although not all, of those considerations are described here. They are listed in alphabetical order. A firm should select those that hold real value and meaning in light of its culture.

Client Retention

Client retention involves the maintenance of good client relations and service, even if little work is actually performed by the individual. Responsibility for maintaining the client relationship and growing that client's business is acknowledged as a critical element for survival in a competitive market. Many law firms reward the "billing" or "responsible" partner for this client retention function based on fee collections from work done by others. Others assess the growth in numbers of clients, matters per client, dollars per client, or total dollars. Still others rely on feedback from clients. This client focus is an emerging trend. Clients are increasingly having input into compensation evaluations (as discussed later in this chapter).

Cooperativeness

Cooperativeness includes the willingness to pitch in when needed, adherence to policies and procedures, and overall demeanor. Those law firms seeking to foster a team orientation stress these traits. Practicing law is stressful enough; the firm does not need the added stress of "Lone Rangers," that is, inconsiderate tyrants or abusive egotists. Creating internal harmony—meaning a sense that the firm will pull together to meet the challenges and demands facing it—is gaining in importance in compensation decisions.

---

2. *Compensation Systems in Private Law Firms* (Newton Square, Pennsylvania: Altman Weil Pensa Publications, 1993).

Firm Management

Another criterion is the contribution to firm or practice management, including such services as acting as the firm's managing partner, serving on committees, chairing a practice department, recruiting and training professional employees, and the like. Good management requires time and effort—the same time and effort one would otherwise devote to fee-paying clients (although most managing partners still achieve impressive numbers for working, billing, and originating fee credits). The firm's recognition of the importance of management and the sacrifices made by good managers is crucial.

As firms grow, management functions become more centralized. This is necessary to carry out the functions of the firm in an orderly manner. Centralizing management responsibilities in one or a few people requires a reduction in their contributions elsewhere. This is especially true for managing partners. In addition, while compensation issues arise in valuing the management contributions of a sitting managing partner, they also arise during a partner's transition from management back into practice or retirement.

Many managing partners devote years to tending to the firm's welfare. When it comes time to turn over the reins of authority, they often find that they have watched (and assisted in) the transfer of their practices to other members of the firm. They may be only sixty years old yet may have a substantially reduced practice. Rebuilding at that age is not a prospect thought of fondly. Failure to consider this typical scenario makes it harder to get old management out and sends the best of the next generation running for cover.

Legal Expertise

Legal expertise refers to the quality and timeliness of work product and advice, particularly if the expertise is outstanding and the lawyer serves as a resource for others within the firm and legal community. Someone once said they could not define quality, but they could identify unacceptable work product, service, or advice. The following definition, however, used by a client of Altman Weil Pensa, is particularly appropriate:

> Quality includes knowledge of applicable law, imagination, creativity and innovation, the ability to write clearly and persuasively, the ability to analyze quickly and accurately, good judgment, the ability to plan and implement legal strategies, good oral communication skills, the ability to handle the unexpected, the ability to negotiate, and the ability to handle complex matters.

Productivity

Productivity is the concept that encompasses the totality of a partner's contributions to the firm and its clients. Partner productivity goes way beyond the numbers generated from the firm's time and billing system. It includes the efficiency with which assignments are carried out, the quantity and complexity of work handled, the number of lawyers supervised, the time invested in training, and other firm activities. Productivity is a term that goes beyond mere hours or fees.

Professional or Community Involvement

Another criterion is the lawyer's involvement in activities such as teaching, writing, and speaking to further education on the law; service in volunteer, charitable, religious, educational, political, and bar and other professional organizations; and pro bono legal work. Such activities do not directly translate into fee revenues. However, the experience gained in leadership and advocacy skills, the exposure to business and civic leaders, and the involvement in one's community all enhance the well-being of the lawyer, the firm, and the community at large.

Seniority

As we know, lawyers take clients and leave firms all the time. The 1980s brought "free agency" to the legal profession. Partners with significant books of business often feel free to market their practices to the highest bidder, one who can also provide the resources needed to keep clients happy. A key aspect of the strength of any organization is its heritage and stability. Such features are gaining increasing importance not only to clients who quickly tire of following their lawyer from firm to firm, but also to lenders and landlords who recognize the importance of those traits in securing the repayment of long-term obligations.

Seniority encompasses more than just age or the number of years at a firm. One New England partnership broadly defined seniority to include the "number of years the partner has spent developing and maintaining clients, building and enhancing the firm's reputation, and participating in the training and development of a cadre of lawyers who produce for the benefit of all the partners in the firm."

Keeping a law firm together for the long haul requires loyalty to the organization. It also requires the organization to recognize the potential for, and to capitalize on, the value that can be added by senior members of the firm.

OBJECTIVE CRITERIA

Objective criteria stress accountability for the organization's financial results. As stated earlier, no compensation system can survive if the underlying economics of the firm are inadequate. It is imperative that any system include some basic economic performance standards in the compensation process. Moreover, the use of "hard" numbers from the accounting system can add credibility and reduce the impact of individual personalities on compensation decisions. These criteria are discussed in alphabetical order.

Book of Business

The lawyer's book of business translates to the "making of rain." For most lawyers it is a struggle to generate business sufficient to be considered a true rainmaker. The critical definition today is that a rainmaker must be a net exporter of work. That is, the individual generates sufficient work to require the employment of others to handle the overflow. Without this, there is little reason for law firms to exist. This criterion is measured by fees collected, usually on an originating lawyer basis. Some firms measure this at a client level, while some measure it at a matter level. The definition of what constitutes origination requires some thought. There are issues of "extended family" origination, "but-for" origination, and "hunting as a pack." In addition, one must decide for how long origination should be credited. There are differing thoughts ranging from the life of a single matter to a set three- to seven-year sunset to a lifetime annuity.

Ask the average lawyer in America today what the most important aspect of future well-being in the profession is and the lawyer will almost invariably say, "Develop an independent book of business." Rainmaking has become the essential attribute to future success. It is, in many respects, the admission ticket to ownership in a law firm. The impact that this has on clients has not been overlooked. Clients increasingly regard an emphasis on origination as contrary to their best interests and have in some instances voiced that concern to law firms (i.e., the client has a vested interest in the individuals who know them and do the work).

Business Managed

Business managed refers to case responsibility and is typically measured on a billing lawyer basis. Growth in this number is achieved through leverage of work to associates and legal assistants. It requires the delegation to and supervision of others.

Hours Worked

Hours worked are most often measured as billable hours. Some firms include "firm" billables, that is, assigned firm projects or responsibilities that are to be considered compensable. Another measurement is to view the total effort someone is making toward the organization. This encompasses efforts and results. Hours worked will remain important in an era of fixed-fee pricing as a measure of time commitment to the organization.

Personal Fees Collected

Another important criterion is the fees for the substantive legal work performed by an individual that are actually collected by the firm. This is the essence of financial contributions. The practice of law requires the delivery of legal services. Very few lawyers can sustain a significant compensation absent a meaningful contribution to personal working lawyer fee receipts.

Realization

Realization refers to the efficiency of turning time into billings and billings into dollars. This is not how quickly one converts effort into dollars, although the two are generally tied together.

Work in Progress and Accounts Receivable

An additional criterion is the value of work in progress (WIP) and accounts receivable (AR). This figure can measure the average age or absolute dollars carried in inventory.

HOW MANAGED SYSTEMS WORK

Managed compensation systems are active tools used by the firm's management to drive and manage change in the organization. The problem with many compensation systems is that they are not tied to the organization's goals, they are not consistent with the clients' needs, and they are left to affect behavior without conscious consideration of the consequences.

Managed systems begin with a plan. The plan defines the behavior required to achieve desired results. Individual plans are prepared that delineate individual contribution responsibility. These plans may be reviewed and incorporated as part of practice area or office plans. Ultimately, the plans are consolidated into the firm's strategic plan to ensure that the various component plans are "in balance" across the organization. These plans do more than quantify the number of hours one will work or the fees one expects to generate. They talk about how the individual will enhance client relationships, build new business relationships, expand personal and firm skills, improve the firm's image in the community, and the like. They speak to an individual's contributions to institutional growth as well as personal growth.

Managed systems seek to instill an entrepreneurial spirit. Thus, merit-based compensation is in and entitlement is out. Merit is determined by performance both in absolute terms and relative to the individual plans just described. This process is the performance review.

Law firms are just beginning to adopt the corporate philosophy of "360° evaluations." This method seeks input on performance from all who interact with the individual being evaluated or who are affected by what that person does. For a partner, this would include other partners (peer evaluation); associates, legal assistants, and staff (upward evaluation); firm, practice, and office management (downward evaluation); and clients (external evaluation). In addition, each individual completes a self-evaluation.

Managed systems recognize a long-term perspective by looking at multiple years of performance as well as the most recent year's contribution. In so doing, they acknowledge the reality of a continuum of performance, mitigating unusually high- or low-performance years and assessing the cumulative impact of individual efforts over the years.

Modern reward systems do place more money at risk. This is appropriate for several reasons.

- Conservative salary or draw helps manage cash flow during the year.
- Salaries and draws are perceived as entitlements. Keeping them low and placing greater amounts of cash compensation at risk reinforces the concept of entrepreneurial effort (i.e., merit).
- Conservative salary or draw provides for larger year-end rewards, which means that those rewards have greater impact and permit management to differentiate appropriately based on performance.

Because these systems tend to be more "active" than "passive," they require greater partner involvement. Working through the subjective criteria can be a daunting task. Objective measures, on the other hand, are generated by the computer (with, it is hoped, some degree of accuracy in their portrayal) and, if accepted by the lawyers, used to add impartiality to the process.

How do law firms deal with the subjective issues? Some firms approach them in a democratic manner. For example, each partner is asked to participate in the process. The participation may be in the form of a questionnaire or narrative comments. Partners may be interviewed by one or more members of a compensation committee. Ballots or "score cards" may be used whereby partners provide judgments on other partners' performance in specific areas. Smaller law firms can effectively handle these deliberations in a single meeting. Larger firms may need several months to gather the information and to allow the participation process to work.

Larger firms tend to use a committee to perform the evaluation (absent complete, formal participation by each partner). Compensation committees are generally a part of or appointed by management. In practice, these committees typically test the waters to ensure that their general thinking is in keeping with that of the firm generally. Their charge is often to make compensation recommendations to the ownership group as a whole. In that capacity, it is critical that the compensation report not contain surprises.

When scoring systems are used, the firm is actually quantifying the subjective factors to provide a methodical way in which to develop compensation decisions and then to integrate them with the objective criteria. Following are scoring techniques that firms may wish to consider if their own system is not working as well as desired. After complete analysis of scoring and computer-generated data, most systems provide for additional adjustment so that inappropriate results are avoided.

- **Ballots:** A ballot system develops rankings by scoring each partner's performance in enumerated areas. Ballots are usually secret. Scoring is often on a scale of one to ten (but any scale will work).
- **Olympic scoring:** This is a ballot approach in which the high and low scores are rejected and the remaining scores are averaged. Such a scoring system is useful in offsetting the problem of "outliers." Determining the median value instead of the average also works, but that figure is more difficult to calculate in large firms.
- **Point accumulation:** This is a "score card" system. Each attribute can have a different maximum point value. For example, quality of work may have a maximum worth of twenty-five points, training and development of associates may have ten points, and business and development may have twenty points. There is valuable flexibility in such a system, since a firm is able to change the relative importance of factors as the firm's needs change from year to year.
- **Direct assignment:** In a direct assignment system, the partners or committee members are asked to determine each partner's compensation. This method is usually implemented in one of three ways: (1) score cards ask for a dollar figure for each partner, and the total must equal distributable income; (2) score cards asks for a percentage, and the total must equal 100 percent; or (3) each partner is assigned a point value that may not exceed, say, fifty points (total points awarded for a given partner will usually vary from one score card to another).

APPLYING COMPENSATION CRITERIA

How to apportion profit is a complex and difficult question. There are no right or wrong answers. As the authors often tell law firms, setting compensation for partners is more art than science. Managed compensation requires evaluating the individual, comparing the evaluation against the evaluations of all other partners and against the plan, and then relating the determinations to available funds. In this part of the compensation-setting process, the concepts of risk sharing, permitted disparity, and peer group are very important. Each firm will have a different sense of what should be done in these areas. There are, however, common issues to address.

- **Risk sharing:** How much risk should a younger partner be asked to assume? How does that compare to the risk for mid-level and senior partners? In addition, if one's risk is limited, should one's reward be limited as well? If so, would that still be true in high-profit years? These are questions that need to be addressed in a compensation system. Firms today are willing to have greater risk sharing. Incentive compensation has supplanted the annual salary increase as the favorite means to reward individuals.

- **Permitted disparity:** Consider this question: Is the individual making $100,000 truly a partner with the individual making $1,000,000? It is an interesting question. At what point does the disparity between highest and lowest paid partner become so vast that the concept of partnership breaks down? Are there exceptions? Does it really matter? The answers vary. Generally, in firms of fewer than forty lawyers, once the ratio of the highest to lowest paid partner exceeds 6:1, there is a loss of partnership identity. Larger firms seem more comfortable with spreads in excess of 6:1, since their size and operating economics allow for such differences. Often the ratio for the balance of the partners becomes much closer if one looks beyond the first or second highest paid partners. This is a typical pattern in law firms with one or two "superstar" rainmakers.

- **Peer group:** The concept of peer group compensation is simply that, since the compensation process is imperfect, it is not appropriate to have small differences in compensation for partners who have small differences in performance. More havoc has been wrought with compensation differences of only a few thousand dollars than one would ever believe possible. The peer group concept is a means to resolve such situations. Individuals with similar overall evaluations are grouped together, and all are assigned the same compensation. Compensation gaps between different peer groups are usually significant. This strategy is designed to head off second-guessing about small differences in compensation.

As stated earlier, conceptions about what "just" compensation is should change over time as the firm's needs change. They can also change for a single individual over time. As an example, a younger partner who feels badly underpaid at $125,000 while generating $250,000 in fee receipts and who has no book of business may take a far different view several years later when he or she is controlling $700,000 in business and generating $350,000 in fee receipts. Then it is no longer "fair" to subsidize the younger partners who have no books of business—the more senior partner must be paid for his or her book of business and the work he or she is performing.

In addition, a younger partner who has a family, a mortgage, and schooling and orthodontics expenses but little or no savings feels far less generous about compensation apportionment than does a senior partner who is more secure and has fewer financial obligations. Each of these individuals will approach the compensation decision differently. Naturally, each is approaching it from his or her own economic situation.

These different positions are often very difficult to reconcile. To start, one must first develop an understanding of each partner's expectations with respect to compensation. One must then find or create some common ground from which a workable system can be fashioned. Often the assistance of an impartial individual is required, one who can hear all sides, summarize the issues, and direct the partners toward common ground.

CONCLUSION

Compensation is one of the most complex and emotional issues that confront any business enterprise. Economics, psychology, sociology, politics, and ethics are all components of the compensation transaction. Each owner makes a personal judgment about the fairness of compensation based on internal and external considerations. Internally, compensation must be fair in relation to others within the law firm. Externally, compensation must be in line with that of peers. Issues of fairness do more to disrupt business objectives, cause defections, or evoke happiness or despair than almost any other issues.

If there is a universal rule with respect to compensation, it is this: Every compensation system works—every compensation system fails. Systems can run the spectrum from objective to subjective, participative to dictatorial. What works in any particular law firm is a system that fits the culture and personalities of the partners. This means that a good compensation system should be flexible to survive the evolving needs of the firm as well as changing ownership. A system must be embraced by the partners, consistent with their collective philosophy, background, and perspective.

Despite their differences, all successful compensation systems feature two common qualities. First and foremost, a successful system must be fair and be perceived as fair by the partners who are essential to the firm's economic success and reputation. The perception of fairness is critical. Even a system that is fair in objective reality cannot survive if a substantial number of the key players perceive it to be unfair. Fairness should not be confused with satisfaction with one's own compensation. Fairness is measured by a sense of equity in treatment with respect to others and by others. The individual's perception of fairness is defined in light of several questions.

- Do I understand the system?
- Does the system recognize the individuals who contribute to the organization?
- Are the rules spelled out clearly?
- Are the rules followed and applied in a consistent manner from person to person and from year to year?
- Are the compensators individuals who are trusted and respected?

A second quality common to successful compensation systems is that of simplicity. Altman Weil Pensa's experience has shown that there is a direct correlation between the simplicity of a compensation system and the degree to which the wage earners understand how their compensation is determined. This, in turn, goes a long way toward the perception of fairness. Simplicity is the foundation. Each additional consideration or step in a compensation system should be measured against simplicity. One might ask, Is the firm truly gaining an insight into an individual's contribution that is worth the additional complexity?

The difficulty in structuring a law firm compensation system is in selecting the best mix of compensable criteria and the right amount of participation that is consistent with the firm's needs and its culture. A law firm is fluid through time. It changes, and the compensation system needs to function like a good constitution—grounded in good basic principles and subject to amendment only after careful, thoughtful deliberation. The experience and objectivity of an outside expert and the candor of confidential input often work together to evolve a firm's compensation system.

An important event in any law firm is the exchange of individual expectations with respect to compensation.

- What are our objectives? Are they formal or informal?
- How much money is enough?
- How much money is not enough?
- What does compensation mean, both personally and professionally, to each individual?
- What level of risk sharing should take place?
- How much disparity should exist from top to bottom?

These questions define much about how economic rewards can be fashioned and how they are divided among lawyers. They may even lead to a conclusion that there are partners who can no longer be members of the firm or associates who should no longer be employed.

Changing a compensation system is difficult. First, one must secure buy-in for both the change and the transition from old to new. Few people react well to change. If you doubt this, consider how difficult it has been to introduce computers to the desks of lawyers or to encourage lawyers to bid for litigation with fixed fees. Buy-in is essential. If sufficient numbers of partners and certainly key partners cannot be persuaded to go along, then change will not occur. Second, the firm's systems and procedures must be capable of implementing the new compensation program. Must the required information be collected or is the information readily available? Do new forms or procedures need to be developed? Are people trained for their roles in the process?

Third, all existing compensation systems are bound by history. As a practical matter, there is a limit to how quickly one can introduce change into an organization. With change come certain reactions. Some of those reactions will result in exactly the consequences that were intended, while other reactions will result in unintended consequences. People need time to adjust to new rules, time to break old work habits, and time to build new skills. Implementation needs careful planning and ongoing fine-tuning to ensure that the long-term success of the change is achieved.

Managed compensation is an approach that, admittedly, requires more effort to implement than most of the traditional compensation systems. For many law firms, however, it is the best way to achieve a perception of fairness and to motivate partners to behave in ways that will lead to the success of the firm as a whole.

There are three trends in compensation that will shape the way law firms reward their people in the future. The first trend is to use compensation as a proactive management tool. Compensation systems drive action and change in law firms, and management must ensure that the right actions and the appropriate change are undertaken. The second trend is to link compensation systems to specific business plans for individuals, practice areas, offices, and the firm. Firms in a competitive market are less likely to be successful if they wander aimlessly toward the holy grail of compensation. Instead, actions must be well conceived and coordinated. Tying compensation directly to specific plan objectives focuses actions on agreed-on activities. The third, and most recent trend, is to link compensation systems to client values. Clients understand the influence compensation systems have on a law firm's personnel. It is in the client's interest to ensure that those systems are consistent with their objectives and values, just as it has been important for them to emphasize that alternatives are needed in the pricing and delivery of services. Client-focused compensation, whereby the client's needs are considered and client input is sought, is the next major wave to wash over the bow of the legal profession.

The bibliography in Appendix 6 of this book includes additional resources for information on partner compensation issues.

CHAPTER 7

Leadership in a Law Firm

Robert J. Arndt

As competition increases, the need for leadership increases. The legal profession has experienced an increasingly competitive environment during this and the past decade. All indicators point toward a continuation of this trend, with intense competition from all directions. It follows that the legal profession needs leaders in these competitive times.

Leaders and leadership are needed at two levels within a law firm.

1. By those in positions of firm leadership—managing partners, executive committee members, practice group heads, office heads, and legal administrators
2. By those leading the lawyer-client relationship

While both are critical to firm success, this chapter focuses on those in positions of firm leadership and is designed to help both current and future leaders, including lawyers and legal administrators, to be as effective as they can so that they can lead their firms through this very competitive marketplace. The concepts discussed, however, also apply to the lawyer-client relationship and can benefit lawyers with that responsibility.

Leadership is not easy. Many managing partners say that the concept of leadership is not readily accepted in their firms. The reasons they give are that their partners have been trained to be independent, prefer to make their own decisions (basically, they do not like to be told what to do), want to participate in other partners' decisions, have large egos, do not generally see the value of a leader, are unwilling to centralize any power or decision making, do not understand organizational behavior, do not understand the power of teamwork or group effort, and, in many cases, are familiar only with hierarchical structures and the concept of a chain of command found in the military and educational institutions.

The author gratefully acknowledges the editorial assistance and guidance offered by the following: Kathryn S. Marshall (Past Delegate, Board of Governors, American Bar Association, and my wife); John D. Connor, Sr. (Partner Emeritus, McKenna & Cuneo); Harry S. Lewis (Chief Financial Officer, Brobeck, Phleger & Harrison); and Joan Zinober (Center for The Professions).

The fact that most lawyers (even in large firms) work individually, have had little (if any) training in leadership principles, and have not experienced the synergy that can be achieved through team effort makes this response quite understandable. These same lawyers believe that all they need to do to guarantee their firm's success is to provide high-quality legal services and to collect the fees for those services.

Noted leadership gurus James M. Kouzes and Barry Z. Posner, in their book *Credibility: How Some Leaders Gain and Lose It, Why People Demand It*, suggest that

> even perfect quality of products and services does not guarantee that businesses . . . will be successful in the next century, for constituent demands and expectations will change with time. It is the quality of leadership that will allow these organizations to anticipate and commit themselves to meeting the requirements of future years.[1]

This suggestion applies in spades to law firms. Failure to heed this demand for quality leadership will result in firm failure or, worse yet, mediocrity. Conversely, quality leadership enhances the firm's chances for success in the long term.

Law firms are not exempt from the major changes occurring throughout the business world. The challenge for law firm leaders is not only to be effective leaders, but also to be effective change agents as their firms are forced to respond to the broad and far-reaching evolutionary (some say revolutionary) changes in the business environment.

This chapter is not a substitute for the many excellent books or training programs on leadership. It is, however, tailored to the law firm environment and provides a capsule guide for the law firm leader—help for the fledgling self-developing leader or a refresher for the experienced leader.

WHAT IS LEADERSHIP?

Kouzes and Posner define leadership as

> a reciprocal relationship between those who choose to lead and those who decide to follow. Any discussion of leadership must attend to the dynamics of this relationship. Strategies, tactics, skills, and practices are empty unless we understand the fundamental human aspirations that connect leaders and their constituents. If there is no underlying need for the relationship, then there is no need for leaders.[2]

John W. Gardner, a noted leadership authority, expands this definition: "Leadership is the process of persuasion or example by

---

1. James M. Kouzes and Barry Z. Posner, *Credibility: How Leaders Gain and Lose It, Why People Demand It* (San Francisco: Jossey-Bass, 1993), p. xviii.
2. Kouzes and Posner, *Credibility*, p. 1.

which an individual (or leadership team) induces a group to pursue objectives held by the leader or shared by the leader and his or her followers."[3]

Leadership is really a combination of both of these definitions. Key words to remember are the following:

- Reciprocal relationship
- Those who choose to lead
- Those who decide to follow
- Human aspirations
- Constituents
- Persuasion or example
- Objectives held by the leader or shared by the leader and his or her followers

The ABA Law Practice Management Section's Leadership Activities Board states it as, "Bringing people together to create successful outcomes."

The term "leadership" is often inappropriately used synonymously with the term "management." Management is a *process* including the key tasks of planning, organizing, executing, and controlling. Leadership, on the other hand, is a different and more comprehensive and interrelated set of four essential skills.

1. Envisioning
2. Communicating
3. Inspiring
4. Enhancing self-esteem

WHAT IS A LEADER?

A leader is simply an individual who makes things happen through others. Although many leaders are described as natural or charismatic, leadership skills can be self-developed as well.

Contrary to the common misconception that leaders are only born, most authorities agree that almost everyone can be a self-developed leader. Becoming a self-developed leader does not happen overnight. The process of becoming a leader is an ongoing, individual learning experience for which the individual must be very highly motivated and take a great deal of personal responsibility.

You can judge whether you are successful as a leader by evaluating whether you have a loyal constituency. Gardner puts it this way:

A loyal constituency is won when the people, consciously or unconsciously, judge the leader to be capable of solving their problems and meeting their needs, when the leader is seen as symbolizing their norms, and when the image of the leader (whether or not it corresponds to reality) is congruent with their inner environment of myth and legend.[4]

---

3. John W. Gardner, *On Leadership* (New York: The Free Press, 1990), p. 1.
4. Gardner, *On Leadership*, pp. 28-29.

Becoming a leader requires concentrated effort, but the personal rewards of being an effective leader will far exceed one's expectations. A leader will create a firm that has the potential of greatness in the eyes of all its constituents (clients, staff, associates, partners, suppliers, the judiciary, competitors, the profession, and the public) and will have a sense of tremendous personal and professional satisfaction.

WHY DO LAW FIRMS NEED LEADERS?

Without leaders, law firms (like other organizations) and their people cannot achieve their full potential, will stagnate, and, eventually, will fail. The legal press continually reports examples of poor or nonexistent leadership. Everyone is aware of firms that were once well led and then faltered when the leadership baton was passed.

On the other hand, effective leaders and their leadership abilities take organizations and their people to new heights of accomplishment—well beyond what would have been possible through uncoordinated individual efforts. The legal press and our own experiences also provide ample illustrations of such inspired leadership.

Leaders and leadership are not the exclusive domain of large law firms. Leaders and leadership are found and needed in firms of all sizes. Leaders provide focus, direction, and inspiration. Absent leadership, law firms flounder, fragment in their efforts, fail to achieve their potential, or simply fail.

IMPEDIMENTS TO PUTTING THE RIGHT LEADER IN PLACE

There are two major reasons why it is sometimes difficult to have the "right leader."

Probably the most obvious is that those with leadership skills do not want the job. Reasons for this include the following:

- Fellow partners do not feel that "leadership is important."
- Fellow partners do not want to "pay" for leadership (it has no perceived value).
- The leader fears loosing his or her technical proficiency, reputation, or both.
- The leader did not join the law firm to be anything other than an outstanding lawyer.
- The firm's profit-sharing system penalizes the leader when he or she passes the reins to the next leader.

These problems can be fixed, but it takes the cooperation of the entire partnership.

The other major reason is that no one within the firm possesses adequate leadership skills. This problem can also be fixed by leadership training or by "importing" a leader from another law firm.

THE TIME REQUIRED TO BE A LEADER

There is no magical formula that will calculate how much time a leader will have to spend on the tasks of leadership. The variables include the size of the firm, the "current state" of the firm, the responsibilities assigned and authorities granted to the leader, the leadership skills of others in positions of power, and the goals and objectives of the firm.

Most law firm leaders seem to spend close to 50 percent of their time on leadership tasks. It is also not unusual for firm leaders to devote 100 percent of their time to being leaders.

FALSE LEADERS AND POSITIONS OF POWER

A leader must be clothed with authority or be in a position of power to be optimally effective. However, it does not follow that an individual, having assumed a position of power, is a leader. A position can cloth an individual with appropriate and necessary authority and provide the opportunity for leadership, but that individual must also have the requisite leadership skills to be followed by his or her constituents as a "leader."

Individuals are frequently moved into positions of power for the wrong reasons: technical ability, professional accomplishment, being the most vocal, having the most money or clients, chance, persuasion, coercion, inheritance, or even by mistake. These individuals have the position of leader but skills that fit a different position. In such a situation, the firm is in double jeopardy, believing a leader is in place and having ceased the search for leadership, all while the leadership function is not being performed.

An organization is truly fortunate when false leaders who lack true leadership skills recognize their limitations and commit to becoming self-developed leaders. If these false leaders do not promptly recognize their deficiencies, they will need tough counseling by senior members of the firm or, possibly, will need to be quickly replaced by a natural or self-developing leader.

HIDDEN LEADERS

Just as there are "nonleaders" in positions of power, it is common to find the "real" leaders of a law firm outside of positions of power. They may be senior lawyers or even younger partners exercising leadership by influencing others. While this is not totally bad, it is neither efficient nor effective.

BASIC STYLES OF LEADERSHIP

Kenneth Blanchard, in *Leadership and the One-Minute Manager*, coauthored with Patricia Zigarmi and Drea Zigarmi, suggests that there are four broad leadership styles.

- **Style 1—Directing:** The leader provides specific instructions and closely supervises task accomplishments.
- **Style 2—Coaching:** The leader continues to direct and closely supervise task accomplishment, but also explains decisions, solicits suggestions, and supports progress.
- **Style 3—Supporting:** The leader facilitates and supports subordinates' efforts toward task accomplishment and shares responsibility for decision making with them.
- **Style 4—Delegating:** The leader turns over responsibility for decision making and problem solving to subordinates.[5]

Effective leaders must constantly adjust and match their style to the particular state of readiness of their specific followers in differing and ever changing situations.

In his book *The Empowered Manager*, Peter Block, an organizational development consultant, goes a step farther by describing two basic approaches to leadership: the Bureaucratic Cycle and the Entrepreneurial Cycle (each of which can be used with the four styles previously described).

The Bureaucratic Cycle emphasizes a top-down, high-control orientation and fosters the use of negative politics. Block suggests that this approach "stems from the success that the military and the church have historically had with centralized control and clarity of roles, levels of authority, and the need for discipline and control."[6]

Block further points out that "success is defined . . . as moving up the ladder, gaining more and more authority and responsibility, and being rewarded financially for that effort. People define self-interest in terms of personal rewards rather than in terms of service and contribution to others."[7] He also believes that the Bureaucratic Cycle exists where "an autocratic culture and personal ambition conspire to support behavior that is strategic, cautious, and indirect—in other words, manipulative."[8] In such an environment, the underlying "patriarchal contract, the narrow definition of self-interest, and the manipulative strategies feed and reinforce each other in a way that nurtures a dependent mentality."[9]

5. Kenneth Blanchard, Patricia Zigarmi, and Drea Zigarmi, *Leadership and the One-Minute Manager* (New York: William Morrow and Company, 1985), p. 30.

6. Peter Block, *The Empowered Manager: Positive Political Skills at Work* (San Francisco: Jossey-Bass, 1987), p 22.

7. Ibid., p. 22.

8. Ibid., p. 22.

9. Ibid., p. 23.

On the other hand, he describes the Entrepreneurial Cycle as emphasizing the use of positive political skills that "involve acting with autonomy and compassion in service of a vision" based on people making "a serious commitment to the organization . . . because they want to, not because they have to. The expectation is that people at each level will treat the business as being their own."[10] Success is defined "in terms of contribution and service to customers and other departments. What we offer people as rewards are jobs that have meaning, the opportunity to learn and create something special, and the chance to grow in a business through their own efforts."[11] This approach emphasizes the use of positive political skills where the "organization will operate to support greatness, courage, and independence."[12]

Thus, the first challenge for the self-developing leader is to decide what leadership style and what cycle best suit the specific situation and the current environment of the law firm. For example, the Bureaucratic Cycle may be appropriate for a short period of time in cases where one senior lawyer is leading a large number of very inexperienced lawyers. On the other hand, the Entrepreneurial Cycle is a necessity with lawyers of equal experience and investment. Careful choice of a specific leadership style and use of the Entrepreneurial Cycle are the most appropriate as law firms approach and enter the twenty-first century. Leadership emphasis must be on appropriately respecting those working with the firm and the contribution they can make in helping attain a collective vision.

The Importance of Self-Esteem

The concept of self-esteem is not generally addressed in books about leadership. It may even seem foreign and irrelevant at first blush, but it is an essential ingredient of leadership. It may even be the most important ingredient because low self-esteem inhibits all progress by the individual and the organization, and it yields all kinds of dysfunctional behavior.

The leader's job is to promote and to facilitate practices that make people feel good about themselves and their accomplishments, to create an environment where others within the organization do the same, and to consistently reward all constituents for so doing.

Characteristics of Leaders

Books on characteristics of leaders abound, and they list the following leadership characteristics most frequently:

Abhorrer of status quo	Adaptable
Achiever	Capable

---

10. Ibid., p. 23–24.
11. Ibid., p. 24.
12. Ibid., p. 25.

Change agent	Manager
Committed	Mentor
Confidant	Motivator
Curious	Negotiator
Customer-focused	Objective
Delegator	Patient
Embracer of diversity	People oriented
Empathetic	Planner
Energetic	Politically savvy
Entrepreneurial	Realist
Global thinker	Risk taker
Highly capable	Sense of humor
Imaginative	Task competent
Innovative	Team builder
Intelligent	Trustworthy
Listener	Unwavering focus
Lucky	

Leaders are never satisfied with the status quo. They function in a proactive mode. They lead well-oiled teams, teams that share a set of values and beliefs, and focus joint efforts on shared goals and objectives aimed at attaining a shared vision. Leaders bind diverse groups of individuals together to work harmoniously. Leaders make their people feel good about themselves and about their unique contributions to the organization. Leaders help the organization and its people engender respect among all constituents.

Successful leaders avoid personal stagnation. They are inveterate learners, read extensively, tap into their alliances, continue to hone their leadership skills, listen to others, and are always attuned to changes in the environment.

Above all, successful leaders continue to challenge themselves and their organizations. They carefully monitor their own and their organization's capabilities for responding to an ever changing business environment. They are always effective change agents.

Being a leader is not a simple task. John P. Kotter, a professor of organizational behavior and human resource management at the Harvard Business School, suggests in his book *The Leadership Factor* that "some of the requirements for effective leadership in senior management jobs in complex business settings" (read "law firms") are as follows:

- **Industry and organizational knowledge:** Broad knowledge of industry (market, competition, product, technologies); and broad knowledge of the company (the key players and what makes them tick, the culture, the history, the systems)
- **Relationships in the firm and industry:** Broad set of solid relationships in the firm and the industry; and excellent reputation and a strong track record in a broad set of activities
- **Abilities and skills:** Keen mind (moderately strong analytical ability, good judgment, capacity to think strategically

and multidimensionally); and strong interpersonal skills (ability to develop good working relationships quickly, empathy, ability to sell, sensitivity to people and human nature)
- **Personal values:** High integrity (broadly values all peoples and groups)
- **Motivation:** High energy level; and strong drive to lead (power and achievement need backed by self confidence)[13]

The obvious challenge for someone in a leadership position is visualizing how to become an effective leader, with all the traits and skills mentioned. A self-developing leader will have to design a personal development plan to enhance existing requisite skills and traits, fill the gaps for missing requisite skills and traits, and become facile in effectively using each skill in a blend befitting the circumstances. While one may never gain every leadership skill needed, the objective should be continual improvement of existing skills and continued acquisition of new skills.

FORMULATING AN ORGANIZATIONAL CULTURE

One of the first tasks for any firm leader is to create an organizational culture by formulating a vision, communicating that vision to firm constituents, inspiring commitment from others in the firm, and enhancing the self-esteem of all around. These things are not easy to accomplish and deserve special attention.

Creating a Vision

The process of creating a vision, or envisioning, basically involves anticipating the future. Even if one cannot precisely predict the future, leaders can perform research, talk to people, gain an understanding of current events and their likely impact on the future, reflect on where they are today, and do a little dreaming about the following:

- What they would like their firm, department, or office to be at some point in the future (i.e., a picture or a vision)
- How they would like people within the firm to behave in their relationships with clients, each other, lawyers in other firms, the judiciary, and the public (i.e., behavioral characteristics or values)
- What core beliefs drive them to the vision and values they have formulated
- What specific groups of constituents they wish to serve

During this fact-gathering phase, the leader should determine what outsiders think about the marketplace, the firm, and its peo-

---

13. John P. Kotter, *The Leadership Factor* (The Free Press, 1988) p. 30.

ple. People to talk to include current and former clients, potential clients, bankers, other lawyers, bar association executives, real estate brokers, investment advisors, judges, professors, chamber of commerce executives, accountants, friends, and other acquaintances.

Leaders will also talk to insiders—the firm's "movers and shakers," founders, senior lawyers, and other knowledgeable legal and administrative staff. Lawyer and staff questionnaires, discussions, and interviews are particularly helpful in obtaining the necessary buy-in because those participating will have the view that their thoughts were considered once a vision and set of operational values are formulated.

It may be useful to organize a personal "board of directors" or "kitchen cabinet." Ideally, this "board" or "cabinet" should consist of a diverse group of peers and advisors representing differing backgrounds and interests, sharing the leader's values, and encompassing a variety of functional skills from both outside and inside of the firm. It can provide perspective, continuing counsel, and balance in decision making.

The key steps in formulating a vision for the firm are to conduct market research, to gain an understanding of current events, to reflect on where you are now, and to do a little dreaming about where you want to be. (The topic of creating a vision and articulating it in the form of a statement that can be internalized by the firm is treated in greater depth in the first book in this series, *Getting Started: Basics for a Successful Law Firm*, 1996.)

Communicating the Culture Statement and Obtaining Buy-In

An effective leader's second task in formulating a firm culture is to communicate the vision to those within the organization effectively. The objective of that communication is that the culture statement be fully understood, remembered, and *agreed with*.

Culture statements generally sound fairly straightforward. However, delivering a culture statement only in printed form to constituents in the firm will engender as many interpretations as there are individuals and will diminish the statement's importance.

Providing an appropriate forum to introduce the culture statement to constituents in the firm is absolutely critical. Optimally, each forum will facilitate the opportunity to explain and discuss the culture statement, to answer questions, and to clarify misinterpretations. Multiple forums might need to be held to gain full understanding of the culture statement.

The act of presenting a culture statement to individuals within a firm does not ensure automatic buy-in by all members of the firm. In fact, 100 percent buy-in might not be achievable until those not buying in "move on." It may even be desirable to out-counsel those not buying in, since they will likely be disruptive of vision attainment. The objective is to achieve a sense of a shared vision while sharing a set of key values. What it takes to achieve this end will differ depending on the size of the firm; the extent to which the new culture statement is a significant departure from prior practices and individual constituents' current vision, values, and beliefs; the pressure for change; and the skill of the leader presenting the culture statement.

Buy-in is essential. Without it, effective long-term motivation and implementation (the third leadership task) will not be possible. Most importantly, buy-in and effective inspiration are not possible if there is a lack of trust in the leader by his or her constituency.

Warren Bennis, distinguished professor of business administration at the University of Southern California, suggests that there are four keys to obtaining trust: constancy, congruity, reliability, and integrity. He further defines these as follows:

- **Constancy:** Whatever surprises leaders themselves may face, they don't create any for the group. Leaders are all of a piece; they stay the course.
- **Congruity:** Leaders walk their talk. In true leaders, there is no gap between the theories they espouse and the life they practice.
- **Reliability:** Leaders are there when it counts, they are ready to support their coworkers in the moments that matter.
- **Integrity:** Leaders honor their commitments and promises.[14]

Obtaining Commitment from Those Who Can Make It Happen

The next leadership component may involve only a few people if it is a solo practice, or it may involve hundreds of people if the firm is large. Nonetheless, the techniques used by effective leaders to motivate those "that can make it happen" are the same, regardless of organization size.

Although all recognize that a leader must have someone to lead, that someone or those someones are often referred to as "followers." Gardner suggests a more appropriate term: the leader's constituency. A fine point perhaps, but a much more appropriate term when our effort is directed at empowering people to act instead of telling them how to act.

The key steps to inspiring the constituency are more difficult than the earlier tasks of establishing and communicating a culture statement to the constituency. If there is an art to leadership, it is in inspiring people to commit to doing acts in furtherance of the vision and to act in accordance with the stated values and beliefs.

The result being sought may have been best stated by Kouzes and Posner:

[W]hen people perceive their managers [leaders] to have high credibility, they are significantly more likely [i.e., be inspired] to:

---

14. Warren Bennis, *On Becoming a Leader* (New York: Addison-Wesley Publishing Company, 1989), p. 160.

- Be proud to tell others they are part of the organization
- Feel a strong sense of team spirit
- See their own personal values as consistent with those of the organization
- Feel attached and committed to the organization
- Have a sense of ownership for the organization[15]

What then are the key steps to effective inspiration or motivation? They are as follows:

- Building and maintaining cohesion
- Organizing for results
- Having the right people in positions of power
- Rewarding (appropriately) individual contributions
- Recommunicating the vision and values
- Renewing the culture statement

Building and Maintaining Cohesion

One thing that is common in most law firms is that managing partners have considerable responsibility but little authority. This type of environment places an added task in the hands of the managing partner, that of building and maintaining cohesion among the partners (who often have widely disparate views when it comes to specifics).

It is important to remember that law firms, in many respects, are essentially voluntary associations of professionals who have bonded together to facilitate the achievement of their individual goals. The genesis of these voluntary associations is the development and maintenance of a shared culture—vision, values, beliefs, and constituents. However, as important as culture statements are, they do not address the specifics of how they are to be attained. The specifics are encompassed in the following:

- **A mission statement:** A description of the role of the firm, or the path chosen, for attaining the vision
- **Goals:** Desired long-term accomplishments, or subsets of the mission (generally qualitative and not measurable)
- **Objectives:** Mileposts (generally quantitative and measurable) attainable within a specific time frame (usually one to three years)
- **Strategies:** How the firm will organize itself and deploy its resources to achieve the objectives
- **A business plan:** A description of the tasks and related responsibilities for the ensuing year

The self-developing leader needs to exercise people skills in building a consensus among fellow stakeholders about specific aims and activities of the firm. The problem faced here is how to

---

15. Kouzes and Posner, *Credibility*, p. 31.

get stakeholders to subordinate their individual self-interests for the good of the firm.

Some "leaders" try to use "authority"—that is, "Do it my way." Some try this technique because they are the right age, have the right client base, have seniority, enjoy an outstanding reputation, and are in a position of power. In the long run, this approach does not work. What is required in a professional firm setting is consensus building.

Common techniques for building consensus include retreats, periodic meetings, committees of various sorts, gentle persuasion, lobbying, arm twisting, and sometimes "horse trading." The method selected depends, of course, on the nature and urgency of the issue, the firm's personality, the leader's persuasiveness, and the extent of sharing of vision, values, beliefs, and defined constituents.

Obtaining agreement on short-term issues and day-to-day decision making depends to a large degree on how much trust the partners have in the judgment and underlying objectives of those in positions of power and how important the decision is to the individual partners. This, of course, is an extremely sensitive area and one where the self-developing leader needs to exercise a great deal of sensitivity, common sense, and caution. Allan R. Cohen and David L. Bradford's book *Influencing Without Authority* (John Wiley & Sons, 1990) provides some very useful suggestions and techniques for getting the job done when the leader's responsibilities exceed the leader's authority.

Under ideal circumstances, the areas and levels of authority will have been thoroughly discussed among the partners. If consensus is reached by the partners, the managers responsible for day-to-day decision making will be able to do their jobs without wasting the time of other partners to decide on such mundane things as the color of paper clips to be ordered.

Organizing for Results

Warren Bennis and Burt Nanus, in their book *Leaders: The Strategies for Taking Charge*, use the analogy of an orchestra in describing how an organization can achieve its vision.[16] The vision is a symphony. Each member contributes his or her skills to making it happen, each member knows what others also need to contribute, and all members know who they are and what they must contribute. The conductor is the one who directs and inspires each member to do his or her "thing" at the proper time. This analogy also fits the law firm environment.

Organizing for results involves two separate concepts. The first is structural harmony. Is the firm correctly organized in a physical

---

16. Warren Bennis and Burt Nanus, *Leader: The Strategies for Taking Charge* (New York: Harper & Row, 1985), p. 214.

sense to attain the vision? Are the right lawyers in the right place? Does the firm need to be organized along geographic lines or along practice area lines? Who is responsible for scheduling employees' time or resolving conflicting client demands?

As with the orchestra, everyone should be aware of how each individual's role (including his or her own) fits into the overall scheme of things to be accomplished. This sharing builds cohesion, emphasizes everyone's strengths and the diversity of those strengths, and makes acceptable the concept of rewards based on group performance.

The second concept is delegating. What are the various "jobs" that need to be accomplished to attain the firm's vision, both in the short and long term? Most lawyers are task-oriented. They think in terms of sequential tasks to be completed and then of asking (or telling) someone to perform those tasks. A change in thinking is required to be an effective leader. The leader needs to think and to communicate in terms of results and then to "empower" (or give the tools, resources, and decision rights to) those assigned responsibility for the desired result. This is not to say that the leader will not give detailed directions or provide supervision, but the difference is the focus on overall results, not on individual sequential tasks.

Effective delegation requires having the right people, developing loyalties, inspiring (not ordering), effectively communicating the "job," monitoring in a hands-off manner, providing private and noncritical feedback, and providing the right tools (e.g., training, systems, technology, space).

Having the Right People in Positions of Power

The firm must create an environment in which all the requisite leadership skills can be developed in all members of the leadership team. It may be necessary to develop the leadership skills of those already in positions of power and to evaluate carefully the *skills* of new people being considered for movement to positions of power. Remember, however, that although people must be rewarded for jobs well done, rewards should not necessarily include promotions or movement into positions of power.

In his book *The Six Pillars of Self-Esteem*, Branden points out another factor that should be considered when individuals are selected to fill positions of power. He believes that people attract others with self-esteem levels similar to their own.[17] This means that if firms are to provide the highest quality of service in a highly productive manner, only leaders with high self-esteem should be selected for positions of power because that will dictate the type of people they select to work with them in attaining the firm's vision.

Rewarding Individual Contributions

Management teaching in the past focused on motivating people by using a "carrot and stick" approach, that is, rewards for good per-

---

17. Branden, *Six Pillars of Self-Esteem* (Bantam, 1994), p. 6.

formance or punishments for failing to meet performance standards usually measured by the antiquated method of fee receipts. The negative aspects of this approach are often compounded by rewarding for increased seniority, status, or entitlement when nothing either tangible or intangible is produced. This old approach is too limiting. The more "modern" approach is to reward, not promote, for accomplishment. Chapter 6 of this book covers compensation rewards in more detail.

Recommunicating the Culture

Messages tend to fade in importance in the collective minds of the receivers with the passage of time and with employee turnover. This means that the firm's vision needs to be recommunicated on an ongoing basis. Some organizations do this with catchy slogans, some use quotes on plaques hung throughout the organization, and some use a logo or statue to visually convey a picture of a vision. For example, American Telephone & Telegraph changed its logo from a bell to a picture of the globe to reflect its move from a "Ma Bell" vision to an international vision, and Herman Miller, Inc., one of the most productive and profitable furniture manufacturers in the country, displays in its reception area a statue of a native American "water carrier" to convey the concept of a "servant leader."

The objective is to inspire all to "live the culture" every moment of every day.

Renewing the Culture Statement

Culture statements, although long-term in nature, can become stale because of changes in clients, the business environment, and individuals in the firm. Take, for example, a firm that was founded by a "benevolent dictator" and that expands to include new lawyers having different values and beliefs than the founder. These facts require the founder (or successors) to continue to renew the importance of the firm's culture with the new lawyers or, if necessary, to reshape the firm's culture to embody the values and beliefs of the new lawyers and staff. The objective is that all members of the firm always share the culture.

Organizations cannot be static because clients' needs change, business environments change, and people change. Leaders need to be sensitive to the winds of change and make appropriate adjustments in the structure of the firm to respond to these changes. In addition, different leadership styles may be required in various key positions of power as a firm moves through its life cycle. (See Chapter 1 of the companion book, *Getting Started: Basics for a Successful Law Firm*). Firms must be sensitive to the need for these changes, since failure to respond in a timely manner can lead to firm stagnation or, worse yet, demise.

Enhancing the Self-Esteem of All Involved

Organizations that have people with high self-esteem are extremely effective, whereas those that have people low in self-esteem are dysfunctional. How the organization and its leaders treat people and how its people treat each other can make the difference and separates the effective from the dysfunctional environment.

To achieve an environment of high self-esteem, the leader needs to do the following:

- Reflect on how most people like to be treated
- Create an environment where expectations of treatment of others are known and responded to by all
- Monitor performance
- Reward positive performance

The specifics of how to do these things are a study in themselves. (See *The Six Pillars of Self-Esteem*, particularly Chapter 15, "Self-Esteem and Work," and Chapter 17, "Self-Esteem and Culture," for a more thorough discussion of this topic.)

COMMITMENT, WILL, AND CAPACITY TO ACT

Developing a positive firm culture and having the skills to communicate effectively and inspire people will go for naught if the leader does not have a personal commitment and the will to attain the vision.

The true leader must also have high self-esteem and believe in his or her ability to attain the vision. This requires a fair amount of self-confidence and, undoubtedly, will stretch the imagination of the self-developing leader. A leader needs to do everything he or she can to build self-confidence by study, analysis, and introspection.

Self-developing leaders need to know more about their organization, its environment, its clients, its people, and themselves than anyone else does. The leader must be *the* expert on the subject at hand.

The leader must also have the will (and, possibly, fortitude) to act. Leadership contemplates taking some risks. This may be difficult for some lawyers because it is contrary to much of their training. However, it is essential for a leader to take risks. If the leader is as much of an expert as he or she needs to be, the risks should be minimal. The leader cannot afford to stand back and wait to see what happens or what others will do—patient waiting may be called for, but the leader should always be preparing to execute the right actions at the right time. The leader must be willing to take the risks and must have the confidence that at the right time the right risks will be undertaken and that the right decisions will be made.

SUCCESSION PLANNING

Succession planning is done on the assumption that those in power want the organization to have a life beyond the useful leadership life of the current leader or leaders.

If this assumption is correct, one of a leader's and the organization's key jobs is to find a replacement leader. Time is of the essence to ensure an orderly transition. While the leader's time frame may be his or her retirement date, prudent care of the organization requires that succession planning has been ongoing for some time and contemplates both the expected and the unexpected.

Similarly, the law firm (basically, its movers and shakers) must be sensitive to leadership "winds of change." In addition to staying up-to-date and continuing to change, the firm needs to monitor the performance of its leaders. The firm has a responsibility to itself to do this, by counseling its current leaders and, if necessary, finding replacement leaders. There should be a periodic review of leadership performance by either an internal committee or by a qualified outsider to help ensure that the firm's leadership is viable and effective.

When the firm needs to replace a leader, it must be extremely sensitive to where it stands in terms of the phases of its life cycle. Different leadership styles are required for different phases of a firm's life cycle. Incorrect identification of the phase or picking an individual with characteristics not in harmony with phase requirements may well court stagnation, loss of momentum, or, worse yet, disastrous demise of the firm.

Selecting the right leader also means matching the leadership style to the goals and objectives of the firm's partners (the owners). For example, different styles are needed in each of the following goal situations:

- Maintaining the status quo. This goal can often be best achieved by a supporting, formalistic, or possibly administrative, bureaucratic leader. However, "maintaining the status quo" really means "falling behind" (i.e., unplanned downsizing).
- Improving market position. This goal is best satisfied by either a supporting or delegating, formalistic or collegial entrepreneurial leader who is sensitive to market conditions, client needs, and how to develop partners who know how to market and effectively provide the right kind of services to the right kind of clients.
- Downsizing. This goal is best satisfied by a benevolent dictator leader who is also an excellent manager.
- Improving profits. In this situation, a directing, formalistic entrepreneurial leader with excellent management skills is required.

Generally, the best place to find a replacement leader is from within the firm. Identifying potential candidates, however, is not always easy. Committee assignments, special projects, and community and bar activities often help identify possible candidates. One additional way to make it easier to identify possible candidates is to create a desire within potential leaders to seek out positions of leadership and to encourage them to express their wishes to assume greater responsibility.

For those responsible for identifying candidates, this question often arises: What traits give clues or indications of potential leadership abilities? While it would be presumptuous to try to list all the clues that would consistently lead to selecting the "right" person, the following are some clues for which to look:

- A person others trust
- A curious person who is an inveterate learner
- An individual who likes people and makes others feel good about themselves
- A person who is not satisfied with the status quo
- A person who is open to new ideas and does not have a closed mind
- An individual with high energy and self-esteem
- A person who seeks to be in or usually ends up being in charge
- An individual who gives credit for accomplishment to others
- A person who does not have a "hidden agenda"

This list, of course, is not all inclusive. The key is to build a checklist tailored to the firm's specific needs.

Once candidates are identified (and, it is hoped, there will be more than the number needed), the development process should begin in earnest. Mentoring, appointment to committee chair positions, encouragement to become more involved in community or bar activities, and attendance at special leadership courses are all possibilities for enhancing the leadership skills of potential candidates.

If the next leader does not exist within the firm, there are three choices: (1) select a "caretaker" until a leader emerges, (2) obtain a leader through a lateral partner admission, or (3) begin planning for an orderly merger or dissolution of the firm.

CONCLUSION

Aggressive, sensitive, and servant-oriented leadership is mandatory for all successful law firms. Unfortunately, few firms are blessed with natural leaders. Having the appropriate leader for the firm's particular situation will engender success, while inappropriate leadership styles or characteristics may mean failure and ultimate demise. Therefore, those currently in positions of power have a responsibility to partners, employees, clients, the public, and themselves to ensure the firm has competent leaders.

The tough question is, How can we provide leadership in an organization of individuals who do not want to be led and who do not see any value in leadership? This question puzzles many managing partners and executive directors. The root of the problem lies in the fact that lawyers prefer to act independently, and frequently use profit-sharing systems that principally reward an individual's personal performance, while failing to foster improvement of people skills, improvement of overall organizational results, or both.

While there are no quick and easy solutions to this systemic problem, the potential benefits of effective leadership make it incumbent on every lawyer to do whatever can be done to *begin* the enhancement process. The foundation of the enhancement process is ongoing education coupled with proactive, sensitive implementation. Here are a few suggestions to help get started.

- Become familiar with leadership concepts by reading and talking with individuals experienced in leadership development.
- Evaluate your own leadership skills.
- If the firm is large, present a seminar on leadership skills to the firm's executive committee, to chairs of all firm committees, to all lawyers responsible for client service, and to key administrative staff, being cognizant that it will be hard to be a prophet in one's own land.
- Conduct an internal self-assessment survey (asking lawyers and staff alike about their views of the firm's direction, responsibilities, advancement criteria, etc.) and an external survey of clients (asking how they perceive the firm, its services, and its people).
- Begin formulating a constituency statement of the firm's vision, values, and beliefs.
- Emphasize rewarding for effective use of leadership skills in the firm's compensation system.
- Provide ongoing leadership training to current and emerging potential leaders.
- Consider the use of a "leadership coach" (probably an experienced outsider) to work one-on-one with developing leaders and others in positions of power.

These suggestions offer a place to start enhancing one's leadership performance as an aggressive, self-developing leader, but it is only a start.

The emphasis in law firms must be on *leadership*, not "caretakership" or management only or bayonet-in-the-back servitude. Being a leader is a "learnable" art. Those who find themselves in positions of power must be (or must become) leaders and must continue to enhance their leadership skills and the leadership skills of all those in their firm. There is no other viable choice.

APPENDIX I

Financial Reports

Report	Use
Balance Sheet and Revenue and Expense Statement	Assess firm profitability, current financial position, comparison to budget, comparison to previous year
Aged Work in Process	Analyze unbilled time
Attorney Time Analysis (Billable Hours Report)	Analyze workload for each timekeeper
Billing Realization (by matter)	Analyze profitability of individual client/matters
Gross Fees Collected per Lawyer	Compare billing to collections
Aged Accounts Receivable	Identify potential collection problems and forecast cash flow
Delinquent Time Report	Identify missing time reports
Variances (over and under) Realization by Timekeeper	Analyze effective timekeeper billing rates
New Matters Memo	Determine sources of new business, and check potential conflicts
Cash Flow Statement	Determine where cash came from and where it went to ensure smooth cash flow

APPENDIX 2

Glossary of Financial Terms

Accounts receivable: Includes amounts (fees and disbursements) billed to clients for which payment has not been received.

Average billable hours: Derived by taking total billable hours recorded by timekeeper classification and dividing by the full-time equivalent number of timekeepers in that classification. This allows firms to monitor trends and to make comparisons with other firms.

Average billing rates: Represents the mathematical average of standard billing rates within each timekeeper classification. This is used to monitor the trends in billing rates within each firm.

Capital/paid in capital/stock (net of treasury): Refers to actual money invested (contributed after tax) by the partners/shareholders. Treasury refers to the repurchase of stock by a professional corporation.

Cash distributions per equity partner/shareholder: Measures the actual cash distributed to equity partners/shareholders in the form of salary, bonus, taxes, fringe benefits, and perks, taking into account additional capital contributed/withdrawn and bank loans/repayments.

Debt to equity: Measures the ratio of bank borrowing to the total amount of partner/shareholder equity in the firm. A low debt to equity ratio indicates that the firm is well capitalized and relies little on external sources of financing.

Debt to fixed asset ratio: Measures the ratio of total bank borrowing (debt) incurred to the book value of those assets (fixed assets net of depreciation). It is a relative measure of a firm's dependence on external sources of financing to meet the firm's operating and capital acquisition needs. A low ratio indicates that the firm relies less on bank borrowing to acquire fixed assets.

Debt: Refers to bank borrowing, including line of credit and term notes.

Expense per lawyer: Measures the expenses of the firm on a full-time equivalent lawyer basis. This allows the firm to track its expenses and any changes that may occur relative to changes in its lawyer population.

Expenses (net of disbursements): Includes all firm expenses before shareholder expenses less all client disbursement recoveries. Client disbursements represent costs incurred on behalf of the client both from external and internal sources. Some examples include photocopying, telecopies, and meals. Compensation for associates and other timekeepers (other than partners/shareholders) are included in this amount.

Fee billings: Includes the amount of fees invoiced to clients, after any billing adjustments have been made.

Fee collections: Represents cash received from clients and applied to the fee portion of accounts receivable.

Fee revenue per equity partner/shareholder: Derived by dividing fee revenue by the full-time equivalent number of equity partners/shareholders. This number is used to analyze whether the firm is promoting lawyers to equity partner/shareholder faster than their ability to generate additional fees. Therefore, it serves as a tool to measure the value added by new partners/shareholders.

Fee revenue per lawyer: Represents fees collected on the basis of the number of full-time equivalent lawyers. This allows the firm to monitor trends in its revenue base compared with changes that have occurred in its lawyer population.

Fee revenue: Represents fees collected.

Fixed assets (net of depreciation): Includes furniture and fixtures, equipment, and leasehold improvements. The term net of depreciation (or amortization in the case of leasehold improvements) refers to the accumulated depreciation being subtracted from the original purchase price of the asset.

Full-time equivalent: The basis for all the per lawyer and per partner calculations. A full-time equivalent is an individual employed full-time for a full year. For example, two persons employed full-time, each for six months, count as one full-time equivalent.

Inventory: The sum total of work in process and accounts receivable. This represents services performed for which the law firm has not received payment.

Months of revenue: A measure of the number of months of average monthly collections represented by the balance of fees in either unbilled time or accounts receivable. The lower the months of revenue, the faster the collection process is.

Net income per equity partner/shareholder: A measure of the average income earned by the equity partners/shareholders. This is calculated by dividing net income by the full-time equivalent number of equity partners/shareholders.

Net income: For a partnership, the total revenue less expenses. For a corporation, this amount includes amounts paid to equity shareholders, including salary, bonus, taxes, fringe benefits, and other perks, plus (or minus) the net income shown on the firm's income statement. The goal is to present the data in the partnership accounting form.

Overhead ratio: The percentage of expenses to total revenue (fees, interest, and other revenue). This statistic is important in terms of measuring trends but not as important when comparing one firm to others. Ideally, for a comparison to other firms to be meaningful, compensation for all timekeepers would be excluded from expenses. This would allow the firm to highlight any differences in administrative and operating costs.

Partner/shareholder compensation: Includes salaries, benefits, taxes, and perks. The ratio of high to low is a measure of the spread in compensation. A narrow spread in compensation generally indicates a situation where there are insufficient profits to permit meaningful distinctions to be made between the highest and lowest compensated partner/shareholder.

Percentage over 120 days: A tracking system used in the aging process to indicate what percentage of inventory (unbilled time or accounts receivable) that is outstanding more than 120 days. A high percentage can be detrimental to the firm's survival because of the questionable collectability of the amount. Therefore, firms must make realistic assessments of their inventories and write off items deemed uncollectible. An exception may be when contingency work accumulates in unbilled time with the collectibility dependent on the outcome of a trial or settlement. Efforts should be made to separate contingency work from total unbilled time.

Profit index: A measure of the firm's ability to convert fees collected into profits for the partners/shareholders. It measures the firm's ability to utilize others to generate fees that ultimately produce net income. To calculate the profit index, divide net income per partner/shareholder by revenue per lawyer. The greater this percentage, the better the firm is utilizing its timekeepers to generate revenue (and profits). The most successful firms have a profit index greater than 1.00.

Ratios (weighted): Staffing ratios are used to measure the mix of employees to determine trends in staffing and to compare with other firms. Staffing ratios that are commonly used include the following:

Associates and non-equity partners/shareholders to equity partners/shareholders: Ratio used to measure leverage, from a staffing basis only. Generally, the higher the ratio, the better the leverage, provided that the work is there to support the leverage.

Paralegals to lawyers: Ratio of the number of paralegals to lawyers. It is also used to measure leverage, purely from a staffing standpoint.

Secretaries and word processors to lawyers: Ratio used to measure the number of secretaries and word processors to the total number of lawyers. Generally, one secretary or word processor supporting two lawyers is considered optimal. However, this will vary from firm to firm and lawyer to lawyer depending on the type of law practiced.

Total administrative staff to legal staff: Ratio used to measure the number of total administrative staff, including secretaries, word processors, and other clerical staff, to legal staff. Legal staff includes all lawyers plus the total number of paralegals and other timekeepers counted at 1/2. Generally, a 1 to 1 ratio is considered optimal.

Realization: The percentage of fees collected to the time value worked (at standard rates). There are two components of realization:

Billing Realization: A percentage measure that matches fees billed to the time value worked (at standard rates). The higher the realization percent, the less amount of time value is being written off at the time of billing.

Collection Realization: A percentage measure that matches fees collected to the actual fees billed.

Time value: Measures the aggregate of each timekeepers' billable hours multiplied by his or her standard billing rate. Also referred to as production. This figure is used to calculate potential billable and ultimately collectible fees.

Timing: The duration between the occurrence of two events. An example is timing for collection, which is duration between billing and payment.

Total revenue: The sum of fee revenue, interest, and other revenue.

Unbilled time: Includes the value of all time recorded that has not yet been billed, written off, or a combination of the two. Unbilled time also includes the value of time worked on contingent fee matters.

Undistributed earnings/retained earnings: Refers to the amount of accumulated earnings in the firm (profits) that have not been distributed (paid) to the partners/shareholders.

Unfunded liability: The amount due a departing partner, other than his/her share of unpaid income through the date of departure or amounts contributed to capital. Examples of unfunded liabilities include an entitlement to receive a share of work in process, accounts receivable, or goodwill, and an entitlement to receive a percentage of average compensation received before the departure.

Weighted census: Shows the full-time equivalent number of persons in each category. The calculation is based on full-time employment in the firm. If a timekeeper works a part of the year, for example six months, that timekeeper is counted as 1/2. The census information forms the basis for comparing statistics between firms.

APPENDIX 3
Financial Profile

	1994	1995	1996	1997	% Change 1994–97
Fee Revenue					
Expenses (net of reimbursements)					
Net Income					
Overhead Ratio					
Gross Margin					
Fees per Equity Partner					
Fees per Lawyer					
Expenses per Lawyer					
Net Income per Equity Partner					
Profit Index					
Average Billable Hours					
Partner					
Associate					
Legal Assistant					
Average Billing Rates					
Partner					
Associate					
Legal Assistant					
Range of Hourly Billing Rates					
Partner					
Associate					
Legal Assistant					
Census (Weighted)					
Equity Partners					
Nonequity Partners					
Associates					
Total Lawyers					
Legal Assistant					
Other Timekeepers					
Secretaries & Word Processing					
Other Administrative					
Total Personnel					
Ratios (Weighted)					
Associates and Nonequity to Equity Partners					
Legal Assistant to Lawyers					
Secretary & Word Processing to Legal					
Total Administrative Staff to Legal					

	1994	1995	1996	1997	% Change 1994–97
Time Value (Production)					
Unbilled Fees					
Amount per Lawyer					
Percentage over 90 Days					
Months of Revenue					
Days Outstanding Unbilled Time					
Fee Billings					
Accounts Receivable—Fees (Net)					
Amount per Lawyer					
Percentage over 90 Days					
Months of Revenue					
Days Outstanding A/R					
Fee Collections					
Total Months of Revenue					
Realization Percentage					
Percent of Fees Received from Top Ten Clients					
Client Disbursements per Lawyer					
Partners' Compensation					
High					
Low					
Ratio of High to Low					
Balance Sheet Items					
Fixed Assets (Net of Depreciation)					
Revolving Credit Line					
Long-Term Debt					
Permanent Capital					
Fixed Assets (Net) per Equity Partner					
Debt per Equity Partner					
Permanent Capital per Equity Partner					
Debt to Fixed Assets Ratio					
Debt to Equity Ratio					

APPENDIX 4

Partner Work Acceptance Guidelines

A. Partners may accept new client representation without any type of approval under the following guidelines:

1. The client is advised that work acceptance is conditioned upon completion of the firm's conflict of interest procedures:
   a. Confirm and document that the firm is not involved with any of the parties and does not already represent any of the adverse parties.
   b. For adversarial matters, prepare a memo to all lawyers announcing the proposed representation. List affiliates, directors, and controlling shareholders if a corporation; list all partners if a partnership.

2. The work is in the partner's area of expertise identified in the firm's expertise chart or practice area designation. Partners can accept work in an area outside of their areas of expertise only if a partner who works in that specific area approves the work and the work is to be done by someone authorized to do it.

3. The client is sent a fee letter and confirms the following as a condition of the firm's agreement to do the work:
   a. The work agreed to and the time frame within which the work will be done, if appropriate.
   b. Payment of a cash deposit to be applied to the final bill or returned to the client upon completion of the matter.
      Note: The amount of the retainer requested is a judgment call by the partner. Generally, it is appropriate to request an amount sufficient to cover billings for the two consecutive months that will require peak involvement. In litigation matters, consider also court time and the *potential* inability of the firm to withdraw.
   c. The fee charged for the work, with time charges computed on the basis of the firm's standard hourly rates or other fee arrangement approved by the managing partner.
   d. The client will be billed monthly unless another mode is approved.
   e. The client will pay within 30 days of invoice receipt.

4. The partner completes a New Matter Report, providing all required information. Any New Matter Report sent to Accounting without an accompanying fee letter will be called to the attention of the managing partner.

5. A client will be considered a new client (and a fee letter required) if that client's prior dealings with the firm have not been sufficiently

recent or extensive to allow the partner to reasonably conclude that the client is creditworthy and will abide by the firm's standard fee agreements.

B. Exceptions to the guidelines above must be approved by the managing partner.

C. Accounting will conduct a credit check on all new clients.

D. The managing partner will approve matters involving the following:
1. Fee arrangements that do not meet the firm's standard pricing guidelines.
2. Contingency fee arrangements.
3. A potential conflict of interest.
4. A potentially unpopular cause or client.
5. A cause that significant firm clients might perceive as supporting a business interest in direct opposition to their business interests.
6. Practice areas in which the firm has no experience.
7. One-time representation of large organizations that present almost certain future conflict problems.
8. Minimum dollar amount of anticipated billings.
9. Work from an existing client who has not been paying as agreed.
10. Pro bono representation.

E. To accept work from an existing client, the partner must verify that the client pays invoices as agreed. If the client is delinquent, it is the partner's responsibility to get approval from the managing partner.

G. Exceptions to work acceptance policies will normally be allowed for institutional clients who have prescribed billing procedures that are acceptable to the managing partner.

APPENDIX 5

Billing and Collection Guidelines

A. Except for bills presented at closings, lawyers will prepare invoices within the time frame set by Accounting and will send bills to Accounting for review and mailing to clients.

B. All bills $_____ below or above (write-downs or write-ups) standard billing rates require approval of the managing partner. All write-offs of accounts receivable of $_____ or more must be approved by the managing partner. Client disbursements of $_____ or more will not be written off without approval of the managing partner.

C. Clients disbursements of $_____ or more will be billed automatically.

D. The managing partner will review monthly a schedule of unbilled time or disbursements that appear to Accounting to be past due considering the nature of the matter. The goal of this process is to:
   1. Prevent time and disbursements from aging to the point that they become difficult to bill and collect.
   2. Keep the managing partner informed of unbilled matters.

E. Accounting will automatically re-bill all clients whose invoices remain unpaid 45 days after the original invoice is sent.

F. If an invoice remains unpaid for more than 60 days, Accounting will activate the firm's collection procedures.

G. The managing partner will approve any letter threatening suit on behalf of the firm and will determine whether legal action against a client should be undertaken.

APPENDIX 6

Selected Publications for Strengthening a Law Firm

Allison, G. Burgess, *The Lawyer's Guide to the Internet*. Chicago: American Bar Association Law Practice Management Section, 1995.

Anderson, Austin G., Denney, Robert W., and James, Carol Scott, *Marketing Your Practice: A Practical Guide to Client Development*. Chicago: American Bar Association Law Practice Management Section, 1986.

Anderson, Austin G., Soper, Katherine B., and Munneke, Gary A., eds., *The Lawyer's Handbook, 3rd Edition*. Chicago: American Bar Association Law Practice Management Section, 1992.

Arndt, Robert J., *Managing for Profit: Improving or Maintaining Your Bottom Line*. Chicago: American Bar Association Law Practice Management Section, 1991.

Arndt, Robert J., *A Model Chart of Accounts*. Chicago: American Bar Association Law Practice Management Section, 1990.

Bennett, Joel P., ed., *Flying Solo: A Survival Guide for the Solo Lawyer, 2nd Edition*. Chicago: American Bar Association Law Practice Management Section, 1994.

Bennis, Warren, and Nunus, Burt, *Leaders: Strategies for Taking Charge*. New York: Harperbusiness, 1997.

Blanchard, Kenneth, Zigarmi, Patricia, and Zigarmi, Drea, *Leadership and the One-Minute Manager*. New York: William Morrow and Company, 1985.

Block, Peter, *The Empowered Manager: Positive Political Skills at Work*. San Francisco: Jossey-Bass, 1987.

Braeman, Kathryn M., and Shellenberger, Fran, eds., *From Yellow Pads to Computers, 2nd Edition*. Chicago: American Bar Association Law Practice Management Section, 1991.

Branden, Nathaniel, *The Six Pillars of Self-Esteem,* New York: Bantam Doubleday Dell, 1995.

Coleman, Francis T., and Rosenfeld, Douglas E., *Handling Personnel Issues in the Law Office: Your Legal Rights as an Employer.* Chicago: American Bar Association Law Practice Management Section, 1996.

Coolidge, Daniel E., and Jimmerson, J. Michael, *A Survival Guide for Road Warriors: Essentials for the Mobile Lawyer.* Chicago: American Bar Association Law Practice Management Section, 1996.

Cotterman, James D., *Compensation Plans for Law Firms, 2nd Edition.* Chicago: American Bar Association Law Practice Management Section, 1995.

Coulter, Charles R., *Practical Systems: Tips for Organizing Your Law Office.* Chicago: American Bar Association Law Practice Management Section, 1991.

Davis, Anthony E., *Risk Management: Survival Tools for Law Firms.* Chicago: American Bar Association Law Practice Management Section and Real Property, Probate and Trust Law Section, 1996.

Denney, Robert W., Jordan, Carole, and Yost, Sandra, *Keeping Happier Clients: How to Build and Improve Client Relations.* Chicago: American Bar Association Law Practice Management Section, 1991.

Denney, Robert W., and James, Carol Scott, *Action Steps to Marketing Success: How to Implement Your Marketing Program.* Chicago: American Bar Association Law Practice Management Section, 1991.

Dietel, J. Edwin, Leaders' Digest: *A Review of the Best Books on Leadership.* Chicago: American Bar Association Law Practice Management Section, 1996.

Dimitriou, Demetrios, *Law Office Staff Manual for Solos and Small Law Firms.* Chicago: American Bar Association Law Practice Management Section, 1995.

Feferman, Richard N., *Building Your Firm with Associates: A Guide for Hiring and Managing New Attorneys.* Chicago: American Bar Association Law Practice Management Section, 1988.

Foonberg, Jay G., *The ABA Guide to Lawyer Trust Accounts.* Chicago: American Bar Association Law Practice Management Section, 1996.

Foonberg, Jay G., *How to Start and Build a Law Practice, 3rd Edition.* Chicago: American Bar Association Law Practice Management Section, 1991.

Gardner, John W., *On Leadership.* New York: The Free Press, 1990.

Greene, Arthur G., ed., *Getting Started: Basics for a Successful Law Firm.* Chicago: American Bar Association Law Practice Management Section, 1996.

Greene, Arthur G., ed., *Leveraging with Legal Assistants: How to Maximize Team Performance, Improve Quality, and Boost Your Bottom Line.* Chicago: American Bar Law Practice Management Section, 1993.

Greene, Robert, M., *The Quality Pursuit: Assuring Standards in the Practice of Law.* Chicago: American Bar Association Law Practice Management Section, 1989.

Greene, Robert, M., *Managing Partner 101: A Primer on Firm Leadership.* Chicago: American Bar Association Law Practice Management Section, 1990.

Gumpert, David E., *Do-It-Yourself Public Relations: A Success Guide for Lawyers.* Chicago: American Bar Association Law Practice Management Section, 1995.

Iezzi, John, *Results-Oriented Financial Management: A Guide to Successful Law Firm Financial Performance.* Chicago: American Bar Association Law Practice Management Section, 1993.

Johnson, Kenneth E., *The Lawyer's Guide to Creating Web Pages.* Chicago: American Bar Association Law Practice Management Section, 1997.

Kotter, John P., *The Leadership Factor.* New York: The Free Press, 1988.

Kouzes, James M., and Posner, Barry Z., *Credibility: How Leaders Gain and Lose It, Why People Demand It.* San Francisco: Jossey-Bass, 1993.

Magness, Michael K., and Wehman, Carolyn M., eds., *Your New Lawyer: The Legal Employer's Guide to Recruitment, Development, and Management, 2nd Edition.* Chicago: American Bar Association Law Practice Management Section, 1992.

Miller, Marjorie A., *Designing Your Law Office: A Guide to Law Office Layout and Design.* Chicago: American Bar Association Law Practice Management Section, 1988.

Morgan, J. Harris, *How to Draft Bills Clients Rush to Pay.* Chicago: American Bar Association Law Practice Management Section, 1995.

Nacht, Arthur F., Green, J. Lary, Vandenberg, Richard J., and Hower, Dale E., *Improving Accounts Receivable Collection: A Practical System.* Chicago: American Bar Association Law Practice Management Section, 1990.

Orenstein, Theodore P., ed., *Survival Skills for Practicing Lawyers.* Chicago: American Bar Association Law Practice Management Section, 1993.

Pennington, Catherine A., *Microsoft Word for Windows in One Hour for Lawyers.* Chicago: American Bar Association Law Practice Management Section, 1996.

Pennington, Catherine A., *Planning the Small Office Library.* Chicago: American Bar Association Law Practice Management Section, 1993.

Reed, Richard C., ed., *Win-Win Billing Strategies: Alternatives that Satisfy Your Clients and You.* Chicago: American Bar Association Law Practice Management Section, 1991.

Reed, Richard C., ed., *Beyond the Billable Hour: An Anthology of Alternative Billing Methods.* Chicago: American Bar Association Law Practice Management Section, 1989.

Reed, Richard C., *Billing Innovations: New Win-Win Ways to End Hourly Billing.* Chicago: American Bar Association Law Practice Management Section, 1996.

Robinson, Gerald J., *Quicken in One Hour for Lawyers.* Chicago: American Bar Association Law Practice Management Section, 1997.

Robinson, Gerald J., *WordPerfect in One Hour for Lawyers.* Chicago: American Bar Association Law Practice Management Section, 1992.

Rolston, Berne, *Law Office Staff Manual.* Chicago: American Bar Association Law Practice Management Section, 1988.

Schlein, Carol L., *WordPerfect Shortcuts for Lawyers.* Chicago: American Bar Association Law Practice Management Section, 1994.

Siskind, Gregory H., and Moses, Timothy J., *The Lawyer's Guide to Marketing on the Internet.* Chicago: American Bar Association Law Practice Management Section, 1996.

Tamminen, Julie M., ed., *Living with the Law: Strategies to Avoid Burnout and Create Balance.* Chicago: American Bar Association Law Practice Management Section, 1997.

Thornlow, Carolyn, ed., *Professional Managers in the Law Office.* Chicago: American Bar Association Law Practice Management Section, 1996.

Weishar, Hollis Hatfield, *Marketing Success Stories: Personal Interviews with 66 Rainmakers.* Chicago: American Bar Association Law Practice Management Section, 1997.

Wert, Robert C., and Hattoff, Howard I., eds., *Law Office Policy & Procedures Manual, 3rd Edition.* Chicago: American Bar Association Law Practice Management Section, 1996.

Woodbury, Carol, *Becoming Computer-Literate: A Plain English Guide for Lawyers and Other Legal Professionals.* Chicago: American Bar Association Law Practice Management Section, 1995.

Index

Index

Selected Books From . . .

THE SECTION OF LAW PRACTICE MANAGEMENT

ABA Guide to Lawyer Trust Accounts. This book deals with how lawyers should manage trust accounts to comply with ethical & statutory requirements.

ABA Guide to Professional Managers in the Law Office. This book shows how professional management can and does work. It shows lawyers how to practice more efficiently by delegating management tasks to professional managers.

Billing Innovations. This book examines how innovative fee arrangements and your approach toward billing can deeply affect the attorney-client relationship. It also explains how billing and pricing are absolutely intertwined with strategic planning, maintaining quality of services, marketing, instituting a compensation system, and firm governance.

Changing Jobs, 2nd Ed. A handbook designed to help lawyers make changes in their professional careers. Includes career planning advice from nearly 50 experts.

Compensation Plans for Law Firms, 2nd Ed. This second edition discusses the basics for a fair and simple compensation system for partners, of counsel, associates, paralegals, and staff.

Connecting with Your Client. Written by a psychologist, therapist, and legal consultant, this book presents communications techniques that will help ensure client cooperation and satisfaction.

Do-It-Yourself Public Relations. A hands-on guide for lawyers with public relations ideas, sample letters and forms. The book includes a diskette that includes model letters to the press that have paid off in news stories and media attention.

Finding the Right Lawyer. This guide answers the questions people should ask when searching for legal counsel. It includes a glossary of legal specialties and the ten questions you should ask a lawyer before hiring.

Flying Solo: A Survival Guide for the Solo Lawyer, 2nd ed. An updated and expanded guide to the problems and issues unique to the solo practitioner.

How to Draft Bills Clients Rush to Pay. A collection of techniques for drafting bills that project honesty, competence, fairness and value.

How to Start and Build a Law Practice, 3rd ed. Jay Foonberg's classic guide has been updated and expanded. Included are more than 10 new chapters on marketing, financing, automation, practicing from home, ethics and professional responsibility.

Law Office Policy and Procedures Manual, 3rd edition. This book provides a model for law office policies and procedures. It covers such topics as law office organization, management, administration, personnel policies and benefits, office security and emergency procedures, financial management, technology, and communications systems.

The Lawyer's Guide to the Internet. A guide to what the Internet is (and isn't), how it applies to the legal profession, and the different ways it can -- and should -- be used.

The Lawyer's Guide to Marketing on the Internet. This book talks about the pluses and minuses of marketing on the Internet, as well as how to develop an Internet marketing plan.

Leaders' Digest: A Review of the Best Books on Leadership. This book will help you find the best books on leadership to help you achieve extraordinary and exceptional leadership skills.

Leveraging with Legal Assistants. This book reviews the changes that have led to increased use of legal assistants and the need to enlarge their role further. Learn specific ways in which a legal assistant can handle a substantial portion of traditional lawyer work.

Living with the Law: Strategies to Avoid Burnout and Create Balance. This multi-author book is intended to help lawyers manage stress, make the practice of law more satisfying, and improve client service.

Microsoft® Word for Windows in One Hour for Lawyers. This book includes special tips for users of Windows 95. It contains four easy lessons--timed at 15 minutes each--that will help lawyers prepare, save, and edit a basic document.

Practicing Law Without Clients: Making a Living as a Freelance Lawyer. This book describes the freelance legal researching, writing, and consulting opportunities that are available to lawyers

Survival Guide for Road Warriors. A guide to using a notebook computer and combinations of equipment and technology so lawyers can be effective in their office, on the road, in the courtroom or at home.

Through the Client's Eyes. Includes an overview of client relations and sample letters, surveys, and self-assessment questions to gauge your client relations acumen.

Women Rainmakers' 101+ Best Marketing Tips. A collection of over 130 marketing tips suggested by women rainmakers throughout the country. Includes tips on image, networking, public relations, and advertising.

WordPerfect® 101 for the Law Office AND WordPerfect® 201 for the Law Office. These two guides are for the new and intermediate WordPerfect 6.1 user. Volume 1 reviews creating, editing and saving documents. While Volume 2 delves into advanced editing and automation features. Each volume includes exercises on diskettes. Sold separately.

WordPerfect® 6.1 for Windows in One Hour for Lawyers. This is a crash course in the most popular word processing software package used by lawyers. In four lessons, you'll learn the basic steps for getting a simple job done.

Order Form

Qty	Title	LPM Price	Regular Price	Total
_____	ABA Guide to Lawyer Trust Accounts (5110374)	$ 69.95	$ 79.95	$_____
_____	ABA Guide to Prof. Managers in the Law Office (5110373)	69.95	79.95	$_____
_____	Billing Innovations (5110366)	124.95	144.95	$_____
_____	Changing Jobs, 2nd Ed. (5110334)	49.95	59.95	$_____
_____	Compensation Plans for Lawyers (5110353)	69.95	79.95	$_____
_____	Connecting with Your Client (5110378)	54.95	64.95	$_____
_____	Do-It-Yourself Public Relations (5110352)	69.95	79.95	$_____
_____	Finding the Right Lawyer (5110339)	19.95	19.95	$_____
_____	Flying Solo, 2nd Ed. (5110328)	59.95	69.95	$_____
_____	Handling Personnel Issues (5110381)	59.95	69.95	$_____
_____	How to Build and Manage a Personal Injury Practice (5110387)	39.95	49.95	$_____
_____	How to Draft Bills Clients Rush to Pay (5110344)	39.95	49.95	$_____
_____	How to Start & Build a Law Practice, 3rd Ed. (5110293)	32.95	39.95	$_____
_____	Law Office Policy & Procedures Manual (5110375)	99.95	109.95	$_____
_____	Lawyer's Guide to Creating Web Pages (5110383)	54.95	64.95	$_____
_____	Lawyer's Guide to the Internet (5110343)	24.95	29.95	$_____
_____	Lawyer's Guide to Marketing on the Internet (5110371)	54.95	64.95	$_____
_____	Lawyer's Quick Guide to Netscape Navigator (5110384)	64.95	74.95	$_____
_____	Leaders' Digest (5110356)	49.95	59.95	$_____
_____	Leveraging with Legal Assistants (5110322)	59.95	69.95	$_____
_____	Living with the Law (5110379)	59.95	69.95	$_____
_____	Microsoft Word for Windows in One Hour (5110358)	19.95	29.95	$_____
_____	Practicing Law Without Clients (5110376)	49.95	59.95	$_____
_____	Running a Law Practice on a Shoestring (5110387)	39.95	49.95	$_____
_____	Survival Guide for Road Warriors (5110362)	24.95	29.95	$_____
_____	Through the Client's Eyes (5110337)	69.95	79.95	$_____
_____	Women Rainmakers' 101+ Best Marketing Tips (5110336)	14.95	19.95	$_____
_____	WordPerfect® 101 for the Law Office (5110364)	59.95	64.95	$_____
_____	WordPerfect® 201 for the Law Office (5110365)	59.95	64.95	$_____
_____	WordPerfect® 101 & 201 Package (5110369)	89.90	99.90	$_____
_____	WordPerfect® 6.1 for Windows in One Hour for Lawyers (5110354)	19.95	29.95	$_____

*HANDLING

$10.00-$24.99 ... $3.95
$25.00-$49.99 ... $4.95
$50.00+ $5.95

**TAX

DC residents add 5.75%
IL residents add 8.75%
MD residents add 5%

SUBTOTAL: $_____
*HANDLING: $_____
**TAX: $_____
TOTAL: $_____

PAYMENT

☐ Check enclosed (to the ABA)   ☐ Bill Me

☐ Visa ☐ MasterCard ☐ American Express   Account Number:_____

Exp. Date:_____ Signature _____

Name_____

Firm_____

Address_____

City_____ State_____ ZIP_____

Phone number_____

Mail to: ABA Publication Orders
P.O. Box 10892
Chicago, IL 60610-0892

Phone: (800) 285-2221 **Fax:** (312) 988-5568
Email: abasvcctr@abanet.org   **World Wide Web:** http//www.abanet.org/lpm/catalog

CUSTOMER COMMENT FORM

Title of Book: _____

We've tried to make this publication as useful, accurate, and readable as possible. Please take 5 minutes to tell us if we succeeded. Your comments and suggestions will help us improve our publications. Thank you!

1. How did you acquire this publication:

☐ by mail order   ☐ at a meeting/convention   ☐ as a gift

☐ by phone order   ☐ at a bookstore   ☐ don't know

☐ other: (describe) _____

_____

Please rate this publication as follows:

	Excellent	Good	Fair	Poor	Not Applicable
Readability: Was the book easy to read and understand?	☐	☐	☐	☐	☐
Examples/Cases: Were they helpful, practical? Were there enough?	☐	☐	☐	☐	☐
Content: Did the book meet your expectations? Did it cover the subject adequately?	☐	☐	☐	☐	☐
Organization and clarity: Was the sequence of text logical? Was it easy to find what you wanted to know?	☐	☐	☐	☐	☐
Illustrations/forms/checklists: Were they clear and useful? Were there enough?	☐	☐	☐	☐	☐
Physical attractiveness: What did you think of the appearance of the publication (typesetting, printing, etc.)?	☐	☐	☐	☐	☐

Would you recommend this book to another attorney/administrator? ☐ Yes ☐ No

How could this publication be improved? What else would you like to see in it?

_____

_____

_____

Do you have other comments or suggestions? _____

_____

Name _____

Firm/Company _____

Address _____

City/State/Zip _____

Phone _____

Firm Size: _____ Area of specialization: _____

We appreciate your time and help.

Fold

BUSINESS REPLY MAIL
FIRST CLASS   PERMIT NO. 16471   CHICAGO, ILLINOIS

POSTAGE WILL BE PAID BY ADDRESSEE

AMERICAN BAR ASSOCIATION
PPM, 8th FLOOR
750 N. LAKE SHORE DRIVE
CHICAGO, ILLINOIS 60611-9851

Fold

ABA
AMERICAN BAR ASSOCIATION

Membership Application

SECTION OF LAW PRACTICE MANAGEMENT
MEMBERSHIP APPLICATION

Access to all these information resources and discounts – for just $2.92 a month!

Membership dues are just $35 a year – just $2.92 a month.
You probably spend more on your general business magazines and newspapers.
But they can't help you succeed in building and managing your practice like LPM.
Make a small investment in success. Join today!

☑ **Yes!** **I want to join the Section of Law Practice Management** and gain access to information helping me add more clients, retain and expand business with current clients, and run my law practice more efficiently and competitively!

Check the dues that apply to you:

❑ $35 for ABA members ❑ $5 for ABA Law Student Division members

Choose your method of payment:

❑ Check enclosed (make payable to American Bar Association)
❑ Bill me
❑ Charge to my: ❑ VISA® ❑ MASTERCARD® ❑ AMEX®

Card No.: ____________________ Exp. Date: ____________

Signature: ____________________ Date: ____________

ABA I.D.*: ____________________
(* *Please note: Membership in ABA is a prerequisite to enroll in ABA Sections.)*

Name: ____________________

Firm/Organization: ____________________

Address: ____________________

City/State/ZIP: ____________________

Telephone No.: ____________________ Fax No.: ____________________

Primary Email Address: ____________________

Save time by Faxing or Phoning!

- Fax your application to: (312) 988-5820
- Join by phone if using a credit card: (800) 285-2221 (ABA1)
- Email us for more information at: lpm@attmail.com
- Check us out on the Internet: http://www.abanet.org/lpm/org

GUARANTEED SATISFACTION:
Your membership must save you time, must give you the edge you need to thrive in the increasingly competitive law business – just as it does for our other 20,000 members. However, if for any reason, at anytime, you think we're not working for you, cancel your membership and receive a refund on the unused portion of your membership.

I understand that Section dues include a $24 basic subscription to Law Practice Management; this subscription charge is not deductible from the dues and additional subscriptions are not available at this rate. Membership dues in the American Bar Association are not deductible as charitable contributions for income tax purposes. However, such dues may be deductible as a business expense.

THE SECTION OF LAW PRACTICE MANAGEMENT

750 N. LAKE SHORE DRIVE
CHICAGO, IL 60611
PHONE: (312) 988-5619
FAX: (312) 988-5820
Email: lpm@attmail.com